Author: Martin C. Sexton

Editor: Dick Hales

Cover design by Martin C. Sexton

Publication design by Martin C. Sexton

Sixth edition - March 2016

Fifth edition - January 2016

Fourth edition - September 2015

Third edition - July 2014

Second edition - September 2012

First edition - July 2012

London Market Systems Limited
Apartment 38, 1 Town Meadow
Greater London, TW8 0BQ

Email: info@londonmarketsystems.com
Web: www.londonmarketsystems.com

ISBN 978-1-4717-6405-9

i

This page has been intentionally left blank.

Abstract

This publication will take the reader on a Darwinian journey of discovery; we will examine the principles of designing classification schemes with particular emphasis on the idiosyncrasies of the financial sector. Classifications, taxonomies and typologies in general use (including the likes of ISO 10962, Bank of International Settlements OTC classification, ISITC Settlements and reconciliation classification) and those proposed or under development (e.g. ISDA Taxonomies) are explored. An investigation is undertaken as to the appropriate mechanisms for representing classifications and how they can be deployed.

The potential impact on product design in the light of the new regulatory frameworks (Dodd-Frank and EMIR in particular) is investigated.

The reader should bear in mind that, "All regulatory roads lead to data" and this publication is the Killer App for grappling with the minefield of financial instrument and product classification - the latest must have Sat Nav.

Online classification repository

A repository of supporting material has been provided, comprising a comprehensive set of samples and electronic representations of the classifications, discussed in this publication.

Go to www.londonmarketsystems.com/classifications and the reader will be able to browse, subscribe to updates and download material for use in development and production environments.

List of Figures

Contents

This page has been intentionally left blank.

Chapter 1

Introduction

1. Introduction

A multipurpose globally accepted classification has been as elusive as the Holy Grail. Few people have managed to get to grips with supporting more than a single business context and even when this has been achieved there is always a risk that it will break at some stage either due to its deep hierarchical structure or a lack of semantic understanding.

Prior to continuing, the reader may find it helpful to read the definitions in Appendix B – The Glossary, this will help avoid ambiguity in understanding the terminology used. To summarise some of the key terms, I prefer to refer to a financial product rather than an instrument and use Feature rather than attribute of a financial product, as the latter can be understood to mean either a data item in a database table or an XML document. Also, Feature allows one to encompass more than one characteristic of a product, for example the legs[1] in a derivative product. Thus a Feature may represent a number of attributes in a physical model or definitive terms in a contract.

I have found that the terms classification, taxonomy and typology are often considered interchangeable. However, I use the term, Classification to refer to all Features, both systemic and product (contract) specific that are used in a scheme. Typology for product specific Features and taxonomy to refer to a collection of terms required to identify individual species or financial product type. The ISDA Taxonomies are good examples with each taxonomy covering products specific to the given asset class.

What does this publication cover?

Examination of the business challenges associated with developing classifications. An exploration is undertaken of existing industry classifications and their business contexts as well as the latest thinking behind semantics analysis.

The Status Quo

Most individuals in the financial sector will have had to get to grips with classifying financial products at some stage in their career. Whether to support regulatory reporting requirements, order routing or some other business context, classifications have touched all our lives.

It is fairly common that a new application to invent its own classification as most industry standards are narrow in scope and can be difficult to understand, especially if there are no accompanying design rules available.

Classifications are required in most processes within financial institutions, from the front office through to downstream applications, the list of contexts includes:

- Product search/selection & approval,
- Investment decision making,
- Trade capture,
- Pricing and valuations
- Order routing,
- Confirmations,
- Client valuations & reporting,
- Collateral management,
- Exposure
- Regulatory reporting (trade & transaction),
- Limits and compliance management,
- Clearing,
- Settlement,
- Reconciliation,
- Corporate finance (general ledger),
- Risk management.

---

[1] Please refer to product examples in Appendix C.

One could argue that many an economic crash might have been avoided if financial institutions had had a suitable classification scheme in place and therefore would have been able to quantify their exposures.

The challenge of constructing an appropriate classification is not just limited to the financial sector; although few areas are so significant. It can be seen in all aspects of our daily life. Wine which can be considered an investment product in its own right, tends to be grouped into broad categories too and there is also the requirement to support multiple contexts. For example, a retail supplier will categorise wine as any retail asset manager would financial products, it is not uncommon to have a customers view, broken down by colour/wine type (Red, White, Sparkling or Fortified), region and price, as well as a sales team view classifying by region, quality and customer savviness. One can instantly see the parallels between the two sectors, especially the need to classify the client's level of expertise.

The wine analogy highlights some of the differences in the types of Features in a classification and given that France is one of the main wine producers it is appropriate for the French term, Milieu to be present in the Classification Core Diagram (Figure 1.)

Typologies, Taxonomies & beyond
The term classification is all encompassing, it is sometimes used to mean Typology or Taxonomy. The best way to show the relationship is via a Core diagram, with the Milieu Layer containing systemic and personal interpretation Characteristics and the Typology layer product specific information. The deeper into the core

one travels, the greater the granularity of information, until finally it is possible to identify individual instruments themselves by a combination of terms. This leads to the classification being usable for searching for products with specific traits. This can then be extended to include abbreviated issuer short names, share classes, etc..., thus enabling the creation of a Symbology able to be used for unique identification purposes.

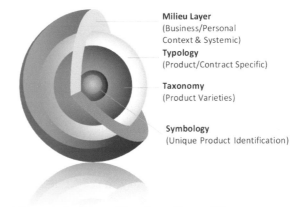

Milieu Layer
(Business/Personal Context & Systemic)
Typology
(Product/Contract Specific)

Taxonomy
(Product Varieties)

Symbology
(Unique Product Identification)

Figure 1. Classification Core Diagram

It is important to differentiate between intrinsic product Features and those external to the product definition (e.g. systemic Features), otherwise one continuously has arguments about how to classify a product. This can be observed when listening to debates about Convertible Bonds, "Should they be classified as an Equity or a Debt instrument?" If one focuses on the Typology, then a convertible has both equity and debt characteristics. It is only when one adds a Business context that one can answer the Equity or Debt question. A convertible is traded as an Equity therefore one may classify it as such and but perversely it pays a regular coupon, so it is appropriate to classify it as debt for portfolio valuation and P&L purposes. There are other non-contractual features that one may wish to capture, these can include how products are settled, geopolitical considerations and capital risk weighting.

Systemic characteristics may include information such as the geographical location where the instrument is traded or the industry sector within which it resides, i.e. the Standard and Poor's Global Industry Classification Standard (GICS®).

Chapter 2

How are classifications constructed?

2. How are classifications constructed?

There are a number of aspects to consider when developing a classification. If one searches the internet, there is a lot of material discussing both the Aristotelian and Dewey Decimal approaches to classifications. However this is not surprisingly the best place to start. The Dewey Decimal scheme was widely adopted for classifying library books and highlights the opportunity to represent a classification in both of human readable form as well as a numeric or codification equivalent. The importance of the Dewey Decimal system will become apparent later in this publication.

Composition of a classification

A classification comprises primarily Facets and Features. With financial based classifications these are mostly code list based. Facets imply a strict mutually exclusive path and, if the node is present, it is mandatory. Facets are "clearly defined, mutually exclusive, and collectively exhaustive aspects, properties, or characteristics of a class or specific subject.[2]"

The ISO Classification of Financial Instruments (ISO 10962 CFI) provides a good example of the use of Facets in the form of the top level "Category" term and its sub category term, "Group", both mandatory, if present. Each Category is mutually exclusive and each Category has a selection of mutually exclusive groups. The Group and Features are on the other hand are optional. Nonetheless their presence provides the opportunity to narrow down to an explicit product type. Using the ISO CFI as the example, each Group has up to 4 Features (or attributes as they are called in the standard).

It may be appropriate to define a large pool of Features from which a small subset is used to define a classification itself. The existence of this collection of terms also has the advantage of enabling applications that require more detail to dip into the pool and extract their specific requirements.

Some classifications deploy enumerated code lists as the case of the ISO CFI whilst other such as the ISDA OTC Derivative products taxonomies are human readable.

Features themselves can be categorised too, as either definitive or informative. Something definitive about a financial product, is a thing that is clearly defined in terms of a contractual definition, such as the holder of the product has rights to receive income or voting rights etc..., whilst an informative feature is subject to interpretation and could be derived by a combination of characteristics. This type of Feature normally results in a lot of theoretical debate at the conceptual level, but from an operational perspective tends to be more clear-cut. A logical model for example, may group instruments by Facet, e.g. Base product, due to the need to be able to work within the constraints of existing technologies, architectures and applications.

The important thing to learn from this is that care has to be taken in designing any classification and clear allocation rules must be defined, especially when informative Characteristics are part of the hierarchical structure.

---

[2] Taylor, A. G. (1992). Introduction to Cataloging and Classification. 8th edition Englewood, Colorado: Libraries Unlimited.

What style of hierarchy structure is appropriate?

There are a number of ways of defining classification hierarchy, either strict or poly. Another possibility is a combination of the two, a multi-dimensional scheme, which I call "matrix" approach. An example of this can be found in the classification based on Asset class and Base product, described in Chapter 23.

Strict Hierarchy

Adopting a strict hierarchy approach means that only a single path can be taken to reach an end node.

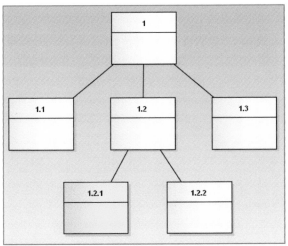

Figure 2. Strict Hierarchy Structure

Poly Hierarchical

The alternative to a strict hierarchical method is a poly hierarchical approach, in which an end node can be reached by multiple paths. Such an approach supports multiple business contexts, though there is a risk of ambiguity unless appropriate rules are put in place.

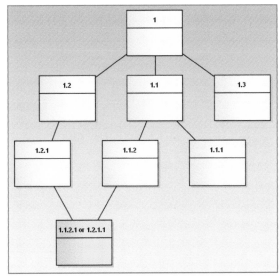

Figure 3. Poly-hierarchical Structure

What pitfalls to avoid?

A clear understanding of the business requirements is essential. Working closely with stakeholders to identify use cases will assist in the task of defining the classification's purpose. A good appreciation of the business and financial products will help as well as the ability to break down terms into their semantic equivalent.

An exercise worth considering is to break products down into cash flows. Having done this exercise, one gets a better understanding of the similarities in financial products. From a classification perspective the majority of Features relate to payout/payoff characteristics. I do nonetheless question whether a cash flow representation gives the whole story. For example, some believe that it is not possible to define a classification without considering the underlying human intentions.

Definition of Characteristics

There is a tendency to avoid defining the meaning of Facets and Features within a classification which results in greater opportunity for a term to be misused. This often happens when the semantic analysis has not been undertaken at the earliest opportunity.

Extrapolating information from existing models can be interesting, given that most terms are defined to meet a specific requirement. To highlight this it is useful to examine, *Option type.* This term is normally used to capture the rights of the holder of the option and contains the values such as "Call", "Put" or "Chooser"). There are other contexts, where this term is extended beyond holder's rights to include product types. For example, this term may be used to represent exchanged-traded option product types, such as Long Call, Short Cut and Iron Butterfly, to name a just a few of the 50+ option products traded on the NYSE.Liffe exchange. Another context is in a swap agreement scenario where one captures the "Payer" and "Receiver", equating a Call with a Payer and a Put with a Receiver option. Combining all this information in the single term, *Option type* will obviously result in misunderstanding at some stage, hence the need to ensure that each term is clearly defined and thus any risk of mixed content and misuse is avoided.

Characteristics should never contain more than one discrete piece of information. There are a number of mixed content examples in the ISO standard (version 2001), in both the hierarchy and underlying attributes. The ISO attribute "*Form*", which contains an indication of the negotiability and/or transmission of the instrument", this has values including: "Bearer" or "Registered" as well as "Bearer/Registered", "Bearer depositary receipt" and "Registered depositary receipt", further proposals exist to extend this term to include "Regulation S" and "Regulation 144A".

A hierarchical Facet containing mixed content can be observed under the Debt category in the group subcategory which contains maturity, product type and issue type related information. These are not always mutually exclusive and if this code list is used in a classification, then it will fail at some stage, even if rules are defined regarding its use:

ISO 10962 Debt Instruments Groups

Version 2001 Entry	Meaning
B = Bonds	Maturity (Long-term)
C = Convertible bonds	Product Type
W = Bonds with warrants attached	Product Type
T = Medium term notes	Maturity (Medium-term)
M = Others (Miscellaneous)	Catch all

ISO/FDIS 10962[3] Entry	Meaning
Y = Money market instruments	Maturity (Short-term)
A = Asset-backed securities	Product Type
G = Mortgage-backed securities	Product Type
N = Municipal bonds	Issuer Type (Entry should reside alongside entries such as Corporate and Sovereign)

In addition, the sub-division of analysis by asset class working groups (a federated model), without a strong overarching coordination of the output can also result in terms being populated differently for each group. In such a taxonomy style approach, the final decision has to be made by the central authority and not the individual asset class user groups.

---

[3] Proposed in the ISO/FDIS 10962, rejected by the ISO community in 2011.

Depth of structure

Classifications with deep hierarchical structures are more liable to break than ones that are shallow, due to the opportunity of a product following two or more hierarchical paths. Having said that if the business rules are clearly documented and the Characteristics defined to an appropriate level of detail, this should minimize the chances of this occurring.

To avoid issues associated with hierarchical design, an approach worth examining is a multiple facetted solution, with the relationship between Facets understood and defined. In addition, any facet in the hierarchy must also have a clear mandate of use. It would make sense for the *Category* to focus on the Asset class (Equity, Credit, Rate, etc...) and *Group* a child of *Category*, the product (Future, Option, Forward, Swap, Warrant, ...)

For OTC Derivative products, a two facetted approach (*Asset class* and *Product*) has been adopted by most industry classifications.

Codification

There is always the possibility that readable entries in lists will need to be represented in an enumerated list form, to minimise bandwidth in information interchange. This is normally achieved by using one, two characters or digits. For example, "E" represents Equities in the ISO CFI standard. Codification would normally be considered where low latency is an essential requirement and would include the pre-trade, trade and immediate post-trade environments. The domain which in operational terms falls under the jurisdiction of the FIX protocol standard.

The Dewey Decimal system is a numerical form of a codification, where products are grouped into classes at the highest level and then sub-divided further to meet the specific user's requirements. The use of a Dewey Decimal scheme can be seen in Figure 4. where a snapshot of a General Ledger classification is provided.

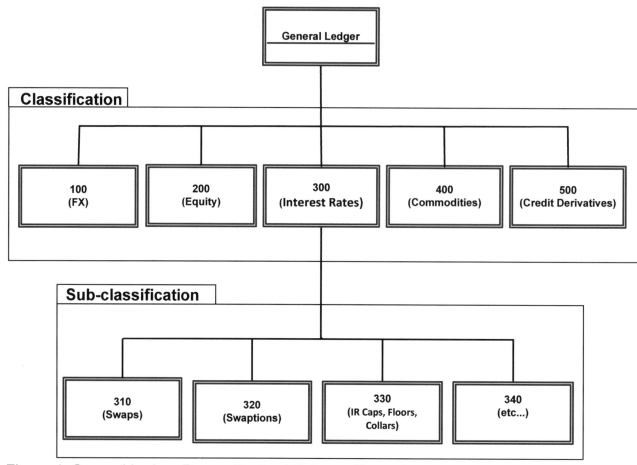

Figure 4. General Ledger Dewey Decimal Scheme Example

The main Base product categories include FX, Equity, Interest Rate, Commodities and Credit Derivatives represented by the values 100 through to 500 respectively, under which sub divisions exist breaking down each Base product into sub-Product groupings. For example, 300 identifies an Interest Rate product and 320 specifies that this is a Swaption.

Chapter 3

Classifications and Unique Product Identifiers

3. Classifications and Unique Product Identifiers

For a classification to be of use there is a need to link it to a Unique Product Identifier (UPI). In the case of the ISO 10962 Classification of Financial Instruments (CFI) this is the ISO 6166 International Securities Identifying Number (ISIN), both are maintained by the Association of National Numbering Agencies (ANNA). (www.anna-web.com)

Identifying a single unique product identifier for the entire lifecycle, across all asset classes, has been the ultimate goal of every financial institution. ANNA has been at the forefront for securitised products by publishing the ISIN, but unfortunately due to the lack of published information in relation to bespoke, bilateral products it has been difficult for ANNA to support all financial products.

A similar model has been proposed by ISDA in the Unique Product Identifier to meet the requirements laid down by the regulators for Swaps Data Repository (SDR) reporting. ISDA has published the Implementation Plan for Unique Product Identifiers. Further information on this subject can be found by going to the ISDA website.

www2.isda.org/identifiers-and-otc-taxonomies/

In the long term, even if ANNA and ISDA coordinate efforts there are likely to still be products that fall through the gaps.

Most organisations have developed their own internal identifier, but this has the risk of persistence if this identifier ends up being used in client systems. Such difficulties have resulted in institutions examining the possibility of developing a symbology solution, where an identifier is based on the Characteristics of the product itself.

Chapter 4

Business Challenges

4. Business Challenges

Most organisations have struggled with the complex task of classifying products for the many different business contexts across the complete lifecycle of all assets.

A particular challenge at this juncture is the need to rationalise the various reporting requirements of the regulators.

The ultimate time bomb ticking away in most organisations is incompatibility between the various classifications used by different applications throughout the enterprise. This disconnection can result in most executive's hearts to race, even more so than Cheryl Ann Cole after an Eliza Doolittle transformation.

The decision has to be made regarding what Characteristics end up forming part of the hierarchical design, by becoming branches nodes, key Features in the classification as opposed to Features in the underlying pool, used for additional information required by applications/services to provide greater granularity to meet deliverables.

The majority of classifications start either with the Asset class or Base product as the top level category. In the past most corporate reporting would have been satisfied by this, however as the regulators and governments flex their muscles there is a need for a classification to drill deeper into identifying the components of the product and its potential for systemic and other risks.

Chapter 5

Financial Products Classifications Landscape

5. Financial Products Classifications Landscape

The chapters that follow examine, warts and all, a selection of the classifications in general use and those proposed to meet the requirements of the pending regulations.

To ensure persistence of the material covered in this publication an online classification repository has been made available at: www.londonmarketsystems.com/classifications

The classifications assessed in this publication include:

- ISO 10962 - Classification of Financial Instruments (CFI)

- London Market Systems ISO CFI OTC products extension proposal (2009)

- Classifications in FIX Protocol

- ISITC Instrument Classification

- EUSIPA (Structured Products) Classification

- European System of Accounts 1995 (ESA 95)

- Bank of International Settlements Derivatives classification

- CFTC Real-Time Public Reporting of Swap Transaction Data; Final Rule (17 CFR Part 43)

- ESMA (formerly CESR) MiFID Classification

- FpML Product classification (Pre-2012 Version)

- FpML Product classification (2011 Proposed)

- ISDA Unique Product Identifier (UPI)

- Accountancy Standards (IAS 32, 39 and IFRS 7/9)

- RIXML.ORG Product Classification

- EDM Council's Semantic Repository

- Financial Industry Business Ontology (FIBO)

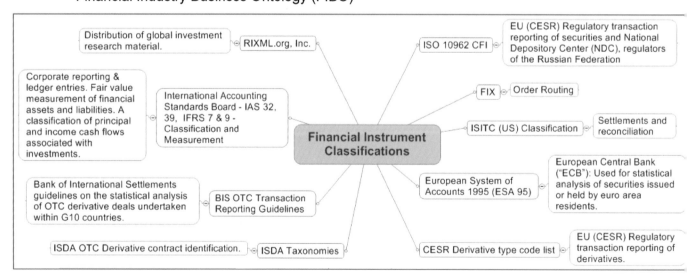

Figure 5. Financial Product Classifications Landscape

Chapter 6

ISO 10962 - Classification of Financial Instruments

6. ISO 10962 - Classification of Financial Instruments

ISO (International Organization for Standardization) is the world's largest developer and publisher of International Standards.

This standard has been around for a number of years and has a vendor centric focus. Designed to be used in conjunction with the ISO 6166 International Securities Identifying Number (ISIN) it is best suited for classifying cash instruments, although it does extend to some exchanged traded derivatives.

The Association of National Numbering Agencies ("ANNA") is the Registration Authority for both ISO CFI and the ISIN.

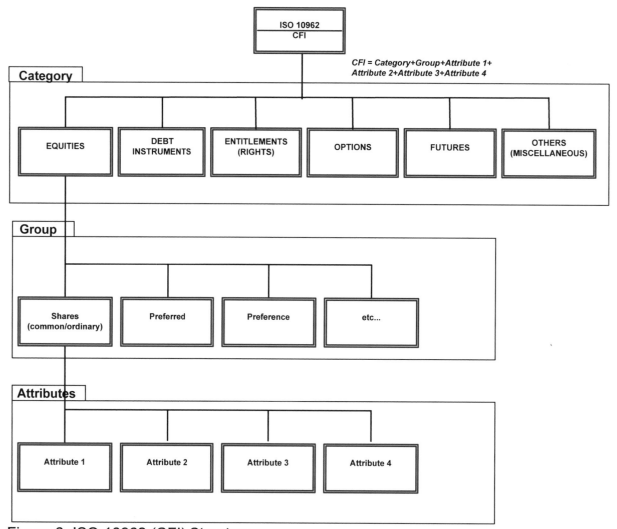

Figure 6. ISO 10962 (CFI) Structure

Version 2001 (2nd revision), the structure shown above, has been the used by the industry for many years. Some regulators have thought it adequate to meet their immediate requirements.

Nonetheless, over the past few years a new version of the CFI was developed by the ISO working group. Early in 2011, it was rejected by the industry, primarily as it was deemed too complex to use. Another reason for rejection of the new version was that a number of the observations raised by the ISO user community had been overlooked. The working group was re-formed in the spring of 2012, hopefully this reincarnation will result in the creation of a fit for purpose classification. The working group is tasked with taking on the recommendations as identified by the ISO study group on identifiers (TC68/SC4/SG1) which in 2011 compiled a set of recommendations for the standard that included incorporating support for OTC derivative products (i.e. the ISDA OTC taxonomies).

Planning for the future

An advisory group has been created by the ISO working group (TC68/SC4/WG6) to address the long term structure and management of the standard, including in this will be the consideration to migrate to a paperless version.

The quantitative analysis, below highlighted some of the positive aspects of moving to an electronic version of the standard:

ISO 10962 CFI Quantitative Analysis

Item	Paperless	Rating (3 Good - 1 Poor)	Paper	Rating (3 Good - 1 Poor)
1 Release Frequency	Reactive, able to keep pace with market changes, depending on Maintenance Authority and data source owner (e.g. ISDA).	3	Normal cycle: 4 years.	1
2 Identification, Versioning, and Maintenance	Can support major and minor releases (e.g. backward compatibility release).	3	Limited to major releases at time of publication.	1
3 Backwardly compatibility	There is a risk of products changing top level categories, if classification based on a large pool of attributes.	2	More controllable.	3
4 Number of attributes	Better control, not limited to 4 attributes, providing the ability to avoid mixed content.	3	Limited (currently) to 4, resulting in the introduction of mixed content attributes (e.g. "Form" has values - Bearer, Bearer/Registered, Bearer depository receipt & Registered depository receipt).	2
5 Code-list management	Multiple code lists can be supported and able to cover asset class/product type variants.	3	Duplicate attributes (using the same name) with different content (e.g. Underlying assets).	1
6 Extensibility	Able to create a greater pool of attributes than the standard. Providing the ability to set category/group from a larger pool of code-lists. Users can create extensions based on the rules defined in the standard. These extensions can be migrated into later versions of the standard.	3	Limited to the details published, the more attributes the bigger the publication. Standard does not include rules to extend.	1
7 Systems integration	Good: Also provides the ability to decouple the definition of the standard from the content and maintenance.	3	Poor: pseudo automated, PDF could be processed to extract material or can be purchased from a vendor.	1
8 Contributions to the content	Provides the opportunity for others to contribute and challenge information, thus ensuring classification is as accurate as possible.	3	Limited to the expertise of the working group.	1
9 Maintenance/Delivery Mechanism	Opportunity to dovetail off over initiatives, such as the LEI.	3	Not applicable.	1
10				

Figure 7. ISO 10962 Quantitative analysis for moving to a paperless version

A number of trade associations have indicated that they are keen to move their classifications to a new version of the standard and thus avoid the need for all the various requirements to be maintained by separate groups and different governance processes.

Version 2015 (3rd Revision)

In 2015, after a number of years of assessment and with contributions from ISITC, FIX Protocol and ISDA, the classification has been enhanced to bring it up to date with the new world of complex financial products.

To achieve this a number of new categories where created and others extended to support the products fall within.

The categories are:

- E Equities
- C Collective investment vehicles
- D Debt instruments
- R Entitlement (rights)
- O Listed Options
- F Futures
- S Swaps
- H Non-listed and complex listed options
- I Spot
- J Forwards
- K Strategies
- L Financing
- T Referential instruments

Users considering migration from version 2001 to 2015 will need to consider undertaking a mapping assessment. Some products have been given new classification codes. For example, Collective Investment Vehicles (CIVs) under 2001 were classified under Equities as Units("EUxxxx"). In 2015, CIVs have there own category.

Issues still remain with the use of the strict "family tree" hierarchy, given that concepts such as "Asset class" and products (contractual styles) are still mixed. For example: an equity asset class product could fall under a number of categories. In the case of products that have Equities underlyers, the fact that the product is equity based is captured at the lowest level of the hierarchical tree by using one of the 4 attribute siblings.

Business context

The current version of the standard 2001 is used in a number of contexts, these include:

- Generally, ISO 10962 classification code is allocated to an instrument and used to identify the appropriate ISIN allocation rule.

- For regulatory reporting, primarily for classifying cash instruments - European Securities and Markets Authority (ESMA).

- National Depository Center (NDC), regulators of the Russian Federation use the ISO CFI to identify the foreign instruments that can be held/traded by residents of the Russian Federation. Only instruments identified under the categories of Equities or Debt can be held.

The aim is to extend the scope in the new version to include:

- Order routing in the pre-trade and immediate post trade (FIX)

- Settlement and reconciliation (ISITC)

- Regulatory reporting/exposure of OTC Derivative products

Online references

Purchase from ISO:
http://www.iso.org/iso/home/store/catalogue_ics/catalogue_detail_ics.htm?csnumber=44799
ANNA Material:
http://www.anna-web.org/standards/cfi-iso-10962/

This page has been intentionally left blank.

Chapter 7

ISO CFI OTC products extension proposal (2009)

7. ISO CFI OTC products extension proposal (2009)

In 2009, the proposal described in this section was put forward by London Market Systems for inclusion in the ISO standard. Since the submission of this proposal, further analysis has shown that the constraints of a single path two level hierarchy combined with the limitation of only four features offered by the ISO CFI design is insufficient to support all the requirements of the complex world of OTC financial products. Nonetheless, this analysis is included in this publication as there are some snippets of useful information, in the form of Features that one may wish to consider when designing a classification.

This proposal has subsequently been superseded by the ISDA and FpML work described in the following sections, which resolved some of the issues raised by this analysis, such as supporting multiple event types and the need to support a Credit Default Swap underlyer.

Financial instruments within scope

All the instrument types identified in the Bank of International Settlements's derivative instrument classification publication, "Guidelines for semi-annual OTC derivatives statistics" are covered within this proposal as well as those identified in FpML and ISDA publications.

However, from a classification perspective it is important to highlight that it is only possible to identify basic cash flow characteristics and constraints applied on those cash flows.

The proposal also examines the Options and Warrants domains within the CFI and provides some recommendations.

The products identified within this report are broken down under into the following groups:

- Interest rate derivatives;
- Inflation Swaps;
- Credit event derivatives;
- Asset based cash flow derivatives:
    - Financial assets.
        - Equity Swaps,
        - Total Return Swaps , ...
    - Commodities assets
- Forwards.

It is worth highlighting that derivative instruments based on underlying financial products are semantically different from those based on commodities (including their legal definitions), therefore these have been separated into distinct groups within the proposal, this also adheres to the current version of the standard.

Interest rate derivatives (category)

Interest rate derivative products define the exchange cash flows of interest payments between parties, typically a fixed rate leg in exchange for a variable rate. They may also include a foreign exchange component.

For interest rate swaps, currency is defined as a characteristic of a rate (Interest/Inflation) swap. To support this, the CFI group subdivides the instruments into 'single currency' or 'cross currency'. Both these groups have the same set of attributes.

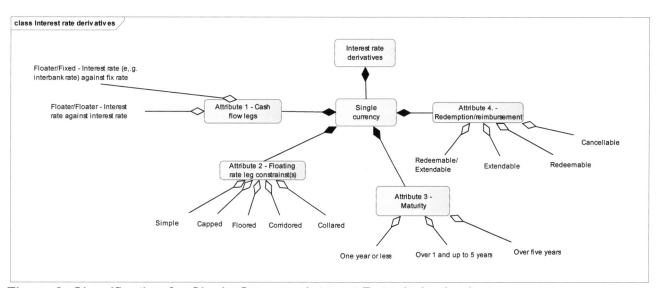

Figure 8. Classification for Single Currency Interest Rate derivative instruments

Attribute 1 - Cash flow legs: classifies cash flow legs (floater/fixed, floater/floater...)

Attribute 2- Floating rate leg constraints: basic constraints on the floating rate leg,

Attribute 3 - Maturity.

Attribute 4 - Redemption/reimbursement: One year or less, one to five years, or greater and whether cancellable, redeemable, extendable...

Example Coding (Interest rate swap)

Assuming the CFI structure is followed, each element would be identified by a single character.

For example: I-S-F-B-S-E

      I = A category of Interest rate derivatives
      S = Single currency
      F = Floater/Fixed
      B = Collared (Both floored and capped)
      S = One year or less (Short-term)
      E = Extendable

Inflation based derivatives

The same structure as for Interest Rates Swaps, please refer to Figure 8.

Credit derivatives (category)

Under this category resides what is commonly know as credit default swaps, these are contracts which commits, normally two counterparties to exchange a periodic fee in exchange for a payment contingent on an event (normally a default).

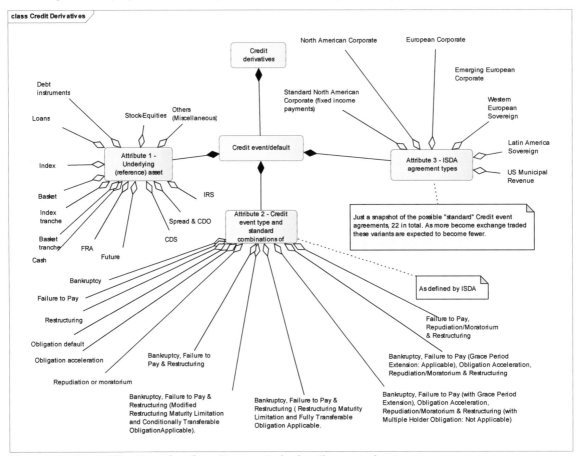

Figure 9. Classification for Credit event derivative products

Attribute 1 - Underlying asset: The type of underlying asset to which the event applies, primarily credit events are against Debt instruments (bonds, convertibles) and loans.

Attribute 2: - Attribute 2 - Credit event type and standard combinations of: Identifies the type of the event(s). ISDA identifies six kinds of events; of which the most significant are Bankruptcy, Failure to Pay and Restructuring. These six are normally not used in isolation and tend to be grouped together in "standard" agreements, hence both the individual event types and standardized groups are covered by this attribute.

Attribute 3 – ISDA Agreement types, There are 22 ISDA "standard" Credit event agreements. As more OTC products become standardised and centrally cleared these variants are expected to become fewer in numbers. Each agreement type represents a standardised set of attributes used (26 in total), which are defined in spreadsheet form published on the ISDA website ("Credit-Derivatives-Physical-Settlement-Matrix…xls").

ISDA CDS agreement types are listed as:

1. Standard North American Corporate (fixed income payments)
2. North American Corporate
3. European Corporate
4. Australia Corporate
5. New Zealand Corporate
6. Japan Corporate
7. Singapore Corporate
8. Asia Corporate
9. Subordinated European Insurance Corporate
10. Emerging European Corporate LPN
11. Emerging European corporate
12. Latin America Corporate B
13. Latin America Corporate BL
14. Japan Sovereign
15. Australia Sovereign
16. New Zealand Sovereign
17. Singapore Sovereign
18. Latin America Sovereign
19. Western European Sovereign
20. US Municipal Full Faith and Credit
21. US Municipal General Fund
22. US Municipal Revenue

Attribute 4 – Unused (and not in Figure 9.) Nonetheless this could be used for Redemption etc…

Asset based cash flow derivatives (category)

These are cash flow based financial instruments where the one party receives payments based on the performance of an underlying reference asset normally in exchange for regular interest payments from the other party. The performance may be a result of the change in value (e.g. price) of the underlyer as well as income, or just one of these two. The payments from the reference asset can be protected against losses (an attribute normally associated with Total Return Swaps). In some instances parties may wish to exchange cash flows associated with the underlying assets that they hold, without transferring ownership of the holdings themselves, these are also supported within this category.

Under this category there are two groups reside, adhering to the same construct used within the existing ISO CFI's Futures category, thus providing a clear differentiation between financial and commodity based financial products.

Financial assets (group)
This group supports all swaps that are based on one or more reference assets (e.g. Stock-Equity, indices, etc...) and encompasses Asset, Equity, Variance and Total Return Swaps.

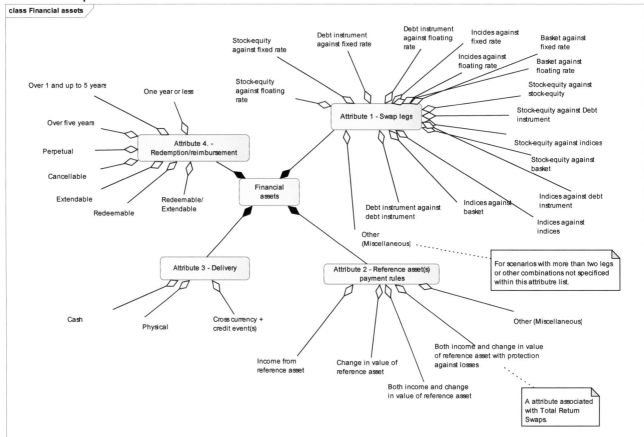

Figure 10. Classification of swaps based on "Financial assets"

Attribute 1 - Swap legs: Used to identify the legs of a non commodity swap. For example, swap may comprise of an equity return paid in exchange for a fixed regular "insurance" payment ("Stock-Equity against fixed rate").

Attribute 2 – Payment rules: Identifies the payment rules that apply relating to the reference asset(s). Payments are based on income, price change in the underlying reference asset, etc... The "Others" definition would be used to cater for scenarios where reference assets are on both sides and different reference asset payment rules apply or for other more complex scenarios.

Attribute 3 - Delivery: Cash or Physical delivery.

Attribute 4 - Redemption/reimbursement: One year or less, one to five years, or greater and whether cancellable, redeemable, extendable, etc...

Commodities assets (group)

Fixed or variable (floating) payments are made to secure the interest in the underlying asset, in return for payments received based on its market price. In some instances this may result in physical delivery.

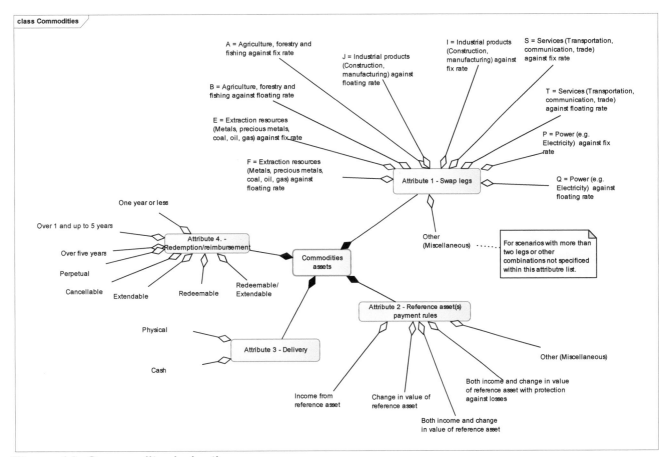

Figure 11. Commodity derivatives

Attribute 1 - Swap legs: Used to identify the legs of a swap where one of the reference asset(s) is a commodity.

Attribute 2 - Identifies the payment rules that apply relating to the reference asset(s). Payments are based on income, price change in the underlying reference asset, etc... The "Others" definition would be used to cater for scenarios where reference assets are on both sides and different reference asset payment rules apply.

Attribute 3 - Delivery: Cash or Physical, this is defined in the 2001 version of the CFI as:

P = Physical *(The underlying instrument must be delivered when the option is exercised)*

C = Cash *(The settlement of the option is made in cash)*

Attribute 4 - Redemption/reimbursement: One year or less, one to five years, or greater and whether cancellable, redeemable, extendable, etc...

Forwards (category)

Forwards are widely used in the OTC world; however the ISO CFI currently only supports Forwards using the 1st attribute of the "Other Assets" Category with the value of M-M-F-X-X-X, providing no details about the forward itself.

The proposal is to create a Forwards category and like Futures, this would be subdivided into two major groups, financial forwards and commodity forwards.

Financial forwards (group)

The classification for financial forwards would be broken down as follows:

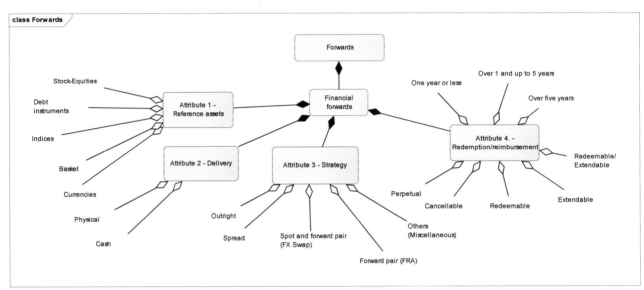

Figure 12. Financial forwards

Attribute 1- Identifies the reference assets.

Attribute 2 - Delivery: Cash or Physical.

Attribute 3 -Strategy: Outright forward, spread, FX Swap (spot and a forward), FRA (two forwards)...

Attribute 4 - Redemption/reimbursement: One year or less, one to five years, or greater and whether cancellable, redeemable, extendable, etc...

Commodities forwards (group)

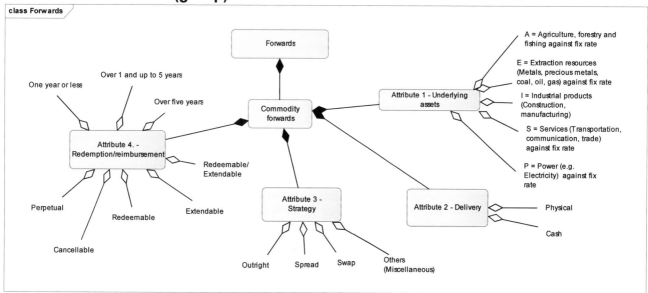

Figure 13. Commodity forwards

This group has essentially the same attribute as financial forwards, however with a different set of reference assets.

Attribute 1: Underlying assets as defined for Commodities futures:

> E = Extraction resources (Metals, precious metals, coal, oil, gas)
> A = Agriculture, forestry and fishing
> I = Industrial products (Construction, manufacturing)
> S = Services (Transportation, communication, trade)
> P= Electricity (extending existing attribute)

The commodities asset classes have been re-examined in the new Asset class classification proposed by the FpML Reporting & Regulatory reporting working group, discussed in Chapter 15.

Option Considerations

Swaptions and Credit derivative options

In its current form, the ISO standard is unable to support swaps, as it assumes that they are either classified a call or put, as they are options on agreements that define the flow (cash or assets) between parties and are relevant to each parties perception (i.e. either the receiver or payer).

Therefore a Swap options category is proposed broken down by the following groups Financial Swaptions, Commodity Swaptions and Credit derivative options.

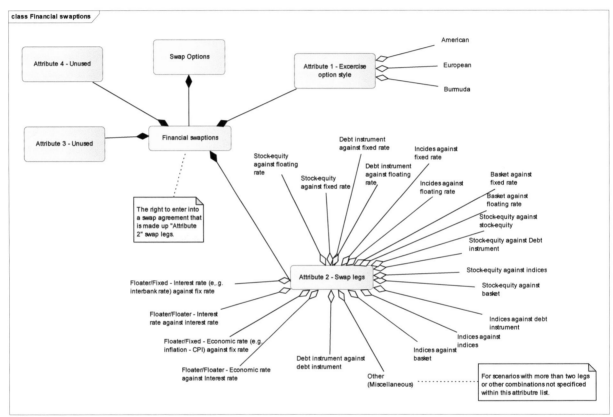

Figure 14. Financial swaptions

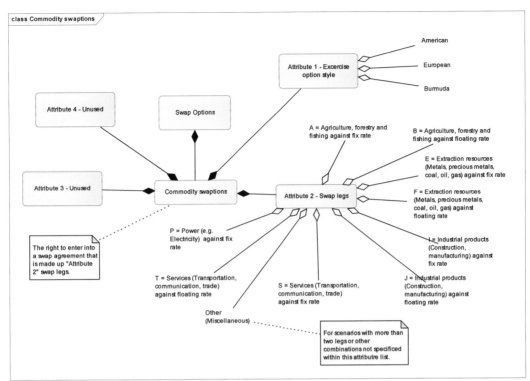

Figure 15. Commodity swaptions

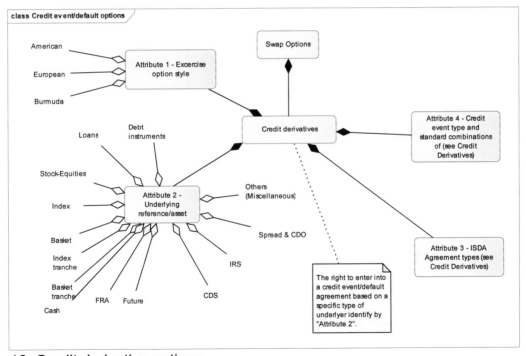

Figure 16. Credit derivative options

Warrant Considerations

There is a requirement to extend Attribute 1 – Underlying assets to include a definition for "Interest rate".

This page has been intentionally left blank.

Chapter 8

Classifications in FIX Protocol

8. Classifications in FIX Protocol

The Financial Information eXchange ("FIX") Protocol organisation comprises a global community of financial institutions and information technology providers that have come together to standardize data interchange between trading partners. This has resulted in the creation of a series of messaging specifications for the electronic communication of trade-related messages.

The FIX community uses a number of data items (known as FIX tags) to help classify transactions in the trading lifecycle.

There are a couple of key reasons why FIX did not deploy ISO 10962 (CFI) standard and took the decision to develop its own classification scheme. Firstly, it can be difficult to allocate the appropriate CFI code, especially when used in the context of order routing. Secondly, the FIX community thought that the Fixed Income asset class was not adequately covered. This resulted in FIX protocol developing a classification mechanism based around a number of tags:

- FIX Security type (Tag 167)

- FIX SecuritySubType (Tag 762)

- FIX Product (Tag 460)

FIX classification – Security type (Tag 167)

Security type is an enumerated code list by which entries are grouped under broad categories, these include, Agency, Corporate, Currency, Equity, Financing, Loans, Mortgage, Municipal and Others). This term is considered as an alternative to the ISO CFI, which the user can supply in CFICode (Tag 461).

It is worth appreciating that similar categories exist as enumerations in the tag Product (tag 460), though there is not a one to one correlation with the Security type, as Security type does not include enumerations to support "Index" and "Commodity" products.

Agency	
EUSUPRA	Euro Supranational Coupons
FAC	Federal Agency Coupon
...	
Corporate	
CORP	Corporate Bond
CB	Convertible Bond
...	
Currency	
CDS	Credit Default Swap
FXFWD	FX Forward
...	
Derivatives	
...	
Equity	
CS	Common Stock
PS	Preferred Stock
...	
Financing	
REPO	Repurchase
FORWARD	Forward
...	
Government	
...	
Loan	
TERM	Term Loan
TD	Time Deposit
...	
Money Markets	
...	
Mortgage	
ABS	Asset-backed Securities
CMO	Collateralized Mortgage Obligation
...	
Municipal	
COFP	Certificate Of Participation

GO	General Obligation Bonds
...	
Other	
MF	Mutual Fund
MLEG	Multileg Instrument
NONE	No Security Type
?	Wildcard entry for use on Security Definition Request
CASH	Cash

There are a number of code list variations that exist in earlier versions of the FIX standard, these may need to be considered as a large number of users are not on the latest version, including:

- FUT - Future(Deprecated in FIX 4.3)

- OPT - Option(Deprecated in FIX 4.3)

- UST - US Treasury Note (Deprecated Value
- Use NOTE) (Deprecated in FIX 4.4)

- USTB - US Treasury Bill (Deprecated Value Use TBILL) (Deprecated in FIX 4.4)

SecuritySubType (Tag 762)
This tag in the FIX repository is described as, "Sub-type qualification / identification of the SecurityType." Therefore if this tag is populated, the Security Type (Tag 167) must also be supplied within a message.

An example, provided in FIXimate is where the SecurityType is set to "REPO" and the SecuritySubType (tag 762) is set to "General Collateral", and is therefore a sub-category of Repo. Another example provided is to use this tag to support derivative strategies, with examples of "Calendar", "Vertical", "Butterfly").

Product (Tag 460)
This tag is primarily used for order routing and is equivalent to the Bloomberg yellow key. The FIX repository describes this tag as, "Indicates the type of product the

security is associated with". The possible values are:

	Description		Description
1	AGENCY	8	LOAN
2	COMMODITY[4]	9	MONEYMAR KET
3	CORPORATE	10	MORTGAGE
4	CURRENCY	11	MUNICIPAL
5	EQUITY	12	OTHER
6	GOVERNMENT	13	FINANCING
7	INDEX[5]		

CFICode (Tag 461)
Nonetheless, even though the FIX community has developed its own way of classifying instruments, the FIX repository recommends that the, "CFICode be used instead of SecurityType for non-Fixed Income instruments."

Business context
Mostly used in the pre-trade, trade and immediate post trade context to support the order routing.

Online references
FIXimate v5.0:
www.fixprotocol.org/specifications/fix5.0f iximate/index.html

---

[4] Not a category in the Security type (tag 167).
[5] Not a category in the Security type (tag 167).

This page has been intentionally left blank.

Chapter 9

ISITC Classification

9. ISITC Classification

The International Securities Association for Institutional Trade Communication (ISITC) was created to facilitate the move towards Straight-Through Processing (STP) and to that end the trade association's Reference Data Working Group has defined a classification scheme to support the post trade domain.

The aim of this standard is to provide a single point of reference for a classification of financial products in a codified form to support settlement and reconciliation processes. "Used for reconciliation proposes, this classification originates from the ISITC North America Reference Data Working Group. It is used in the Settlement Instructions MT54x and other SWIFT messages as well as the equivalent ISO 200022 messages".

The ISITC classification is based on two level hierarchy, comparable to the ISO CFI, though heavily weighted towards products traded in the US markets. The classification code itself is up to four alpha-characters in enumerated form (e.g. "CDO" representing Collateralized Debt Obligation).

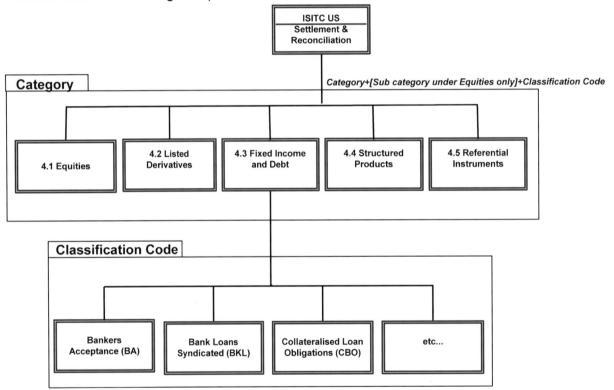

Figure 17. ISITC US Settlements and Reconciliations classification

ISITC has documented the market practice relating to the classification of financial products in settlement and reconciliation messages used principally, over the SWIFT network. The associated terms used in the messaging include 'PSET List Asset Type Code' combined with US Security and SSI Security Type Code. These are all cross-referenced back to the ISITC classification, please refer to Figure 18 for the associated mappings.

The sample that follows is taken from the "ISITC Classification Code List" document (4.3 Fixed Income and Debt category):

4.3 Fixed Income and Debt

ISITC Code		Settlements MP Linkages			Ref Data MP Linkages	Reconciliation MP Linkages (Usage in the Below Messages)				
ISITC Classification Code	ISITC Classification Code Description	PSET List – Asset Type Code	US Security MP Template	Message Type	SSI Security Type Code	MT535 Custody	MT535 Accting	MT536	MT537	MT950
Fixed Income and Debt										
BA	Bankers Acceptance	MM	BA	MT54X	MMKT	✓	✓	✓	✓	✓
BKL	Bank Loans (Syndicated Bank Loans)	EQ	BKL	MT54X	CORP	Not Yet Defined	Not Yet Defined	Not Yet Defined	Not Yet Defined	Not Yet Defined
CBO	Collateralized Bond Obligation	CORP	CLO	MT54X	CORP	✓	✓	✓	✓	✓
CD	Certificate of Deposit	MM	CD	MT54X	MMKT	✓	✓	✓	✓	✓
CDO	Collateralized Debt Obligation	CORP	CLO	MT54X	CORP	✓	✓	✓	✓	✓
CLO	Collateralized Loan Obligation	CORP	CLO	MT54X	CORP	✓	✓	✓	✓	✓
CMO	Collateralized Mort. Obl. (incl. sinking funds)	CORP	CMO	MT54X	MTGE	✓	✓	✓	✓	✓
CORP	Corporate Bond	CORP	CORP	MT54X	CORP	✓	✓	✓	✓	✓
CP	Commercial Paper	MM	CP	MT54X	MMKT	✓	✓	✓	✓	✓
CPP	Corporate Private Placement	CORP	CORP	MT54X	CORP	✓	✓	✓	✓	✓
DISC	Discount Note	CORP	DISC	MT54X	CORP	✓	✓	✓	✓	✓

Figure 18. ISITC US Classification, Fixed Income and Debt category snapshot[6]

There is no embedded logic in the simple hierarchy apart from how the instrument is traded/settled.

Business context

Designed to support the settlement and reconciliation processes and used to tie together the various terms used in SWIFT messages, such as:

- MT54x – Settlement Instructions
- MT535 – Statement of Holdings
- MT536 – Statement of Transactions
- MT537 – Statement of Pending Transactions
- MT950 – Cash Statement
- and the equivalent ISO 20022 messages.

Online references

www.isitc.org/getFile.cfm?f=%5Cmarket%20practice%20documents%5Creference%20data%20%26%20
standards%20working%20group%5CISITC%20Classification%20Code%20List%20v%201%209(a).pdf

---

[6] ISITC Classification Code List - Version 1.9 - Publication Date: February 22, 2011, ISITC Reference Data Working Group

This page has been intentionally left blank.

Chapter 10

EUSIPA Classification

10. EUSIPA Structured Products Classification

"10. European Structured Investment Products Association (EUSIPA) is a European based organization created to promote the interests of the structured retail investment products market. Its aim is to ensure a uniform approach to issuance of structured products across Europe. In November 2009, EUSIPA launched a new classification scheme for structured products. Primarily used in the Austrian, German and Swiss markets, it focuses on the payout profiles of fungible structured and derivative instruments. As well as the German speaking countries the other countries in the consortium include France, Italy and Sweden.

The classification has a simple hierarchy structure and can also be represented in a codified form (e.g. 1260 - Express Certificates). At the highest level, products are categorized as being under either Investment (1xxx) or Leverage products (2xxx).

Under investment products the sub-categories are Capital Protection, Yield Enhancement and Participation Product whereas leveraged products are sub-categorised as with or without Knock-Out.

In addition to the 3 tier hierarchy, products may be jurisdiction specific, in that different legal conditions may apply for the same EUSIPA classification. This is highlighted by the different product name given to products in Austria and Germany; please refer to their respective flags in the classification definition:

1 INVESTMENT PRODUCTS *issues all products*

11 CAPITAL PROTECTION
1100 Uncapped Capital Protection
1110 Exchangeable Certificates &
1120 Capped Capital Protected
1130 Capital Protection with Knock-out
1140 Capital Protection with Coupon
1199 Various Capital Protection &

12 YIELD ENHANCEMENT
1200 Discount Certificates
1210 Barrier Discount Certificates
1220 Reverse Convertibles &
1230 Barrier Reverse Convertibles
1240 Capped Outperformance Certificates
1250 Capped Bonus / Sprint Certificates in
1260 Express Certificates (or 1270 in &)
1299 Various Yield Enhancement

13 PARTICIPATION
1300 Tracker Certificates (Index/Participation Certificates in &)
1310 Outperformance Certificates &
1320 Bonus Certificates &
1330 Outperformance Bonus Certificates
1340 Twin-Win Certificates
1399 Various Participation

2 LEVERAGE PRODUCTS *issues all products*

21 LEVERAGE WITHOUT KNOCK-OUT
2100 Warrants (or Options in &)
2199 Various Leverage without Knock-Out &

22 LEVERAGE WITH KNOCK-OUT
2200 Knock-out Warrants/ Products
2210 Mini-Futures
2299 Various Leverage with Knock-Out &

Business context
Used for statistical analysis of securities issued or held by euro area residents.

Online references
www.eusipa.org/images/grafiken/Ansicht _european_map_280709.pdf

Chapter 11

European System of Accounts 1995 (ESA 95)

11. European System of Accounts 1995 (ESA 95)

Defined by the European Central Bank ("ECB") for use in statistical analysis, this is a hierarchical classification of up to 5 levels in depth. It is used to classify instruments traded on the various European financial markets.

At the highest level the main categories include:

- Interest rate instruments
- Equity-related instruments
- Investment and money market funds' shares/units and related instruments
- Foreign exchange and related instruments
- Commodity derivatives, credit derivatives and other complex derivative products.
- Commodities

The extract below, taken from the ECB publication, "*Statistical Classification*

of Financial Markets Instruments" dated July 2005, shows a snippet of the classification.

2 Equity-related instruments	2.1 Stocks	2.1.1 Quoted stocks
		2.1.2 Unquoted stocks
		2.1.3 Other equity
	2.2 Equity-linked derivatives	2.2.1 Forward-type derivatives
		2.2.2 Option-type derivatives
3 Investment and money market funds' shares/units and related instruments	3.1 Investment and money market funds shares/units	3.1.1 Money market funds
		3.1.2 Bond funds
		3.1.3 Equity funds
		3.1.4 Mixed funds
		3.1.5 Real estate funds
		3.1.6 Hedge funds
		3.1.7 Other funds
	3.2 Derivatives on investment and money market funds' shares/units	3.2.1 Forward-type derivatives
		3.2.2 Option-type derivatives

Figure 19. Snippet of ECB Statistical Classification of Financial Markets Instruments

In addition to the human readable hierarchy, the standard provides a cross reference table to the ESA 95 financial assets codification.

1 Interest rate instruments	1.1 Deposits, loans and debt securities	1.1.1 Deposits and loans	1.1.1.1 [1] Short term (up to and including 1 year)	AF.22 Transferable deposits. AF.29 Other deposits. AF.4 Loans.
			1.1.1.2 [1] Long term (over 1 year)	
		1.1.2 Debt securities	1.1.2.1 Short term (up to and including 1 year) [2]	AF.33 Securities other than shares, excluding financial derivatives
			1.1.2.2 Long term (over 1 year) [2]	
	1.2 Interest rate derivatives	1.2.1 Forward-type derivatives		AF.34 Financial derivatives.
		1.2.2 Option-type derivatives		
2 Equity-related instruments	2.1 Stocks	2.1.1 Quoted stocks		AF.511 Quoted shares, excluding mutual funds shares.
		2.1.2 Unquoted stocks		AF.512 Unquoted shares, excluding mutual funds shares.
		2.1.3 Other equity		AF.513 Other equity.
	2.2 Equity-linked derivatives	2.2.1 Forward-type derivatives		AF.34 Financial derivatives.
		2.2.2 Option-type derivatives		

Figure 20. financial markets instruments with links to the ESA 95

The codes are:

- AF.22 Transferable deposits
- AF.29 Other deposits
- AF. 4 Loans
- AF.33 Securities other than shares,
- AF.34 Financial derivatives
- AF.52 Mutual funds shares
- AF.1 Monetary gold & special rights
- AF.21 Currency
- AF.6 Insurance technical reserves
- AF.7 Other accounts payable/receivable

Business context
Used for statistical analysis of securities issued by or held by Euro area firms and residents.

Online references
Statistical classification of financial markets instruments (2005):
www.ecb.int/pub/pdf/other/statisticalclassificationfmi200507en.pdf

Chapter 12

Bank of International Settlements
Derivative instruments classification

12. Bank of International Settlements - Derivative instruments classification

The objective of the Bank of International Settlements (BIS) classification is to support the creation of the triennial and semi-annual surveys on positions in global over-the-counter (OTC) derivatives markets.

This classification is used to provide information on the size and structure of the global derivatives markets and to obtain an assessment of the risk being traded/transferred in these markets. In addition, to market risk (based on asset class and product type groupings), statistics are broken down by:

- By geo-political regions (North America, Japan, Europe, Latin America, other Asia) for CDS and Equity linked derivatives, as part of the Triennial survey only.
- For all derivatives, by the type of counterparty and sector (Reporting dealers, Central counterparties, Non-financial customers, other financial institutions, etc...).
- For foreign exchange and interest rate contracts, by the major currency pairs[7], as part of the Triennial survey.
- For equity contracts, by geo-political regions.

- For the Semi-annual survey, by time to maturity of foreign exchange, interest rate and equity contracts (under one year, over one and up to five years and over 5 years).

- For the Triennial survey, statistics are broken down by actual maturity.

The two tier hierarchy breaks down transactions by asset class and product type.

Asset Class
Foreign exchange transactions (and gold contracts)
Single-currency interest rate derivatives
Equity and stock index derivatives
Commodity derivatives (excluding gold contracts)
Credit and other derivatives

Product Type
Swap
Forward
Future
Option

Where non-plain vanilla products exist, the guidelines recommend that they are separated into their vanilla components and classified accordingly.

Given that this scheme was designed in the late 90's, it has been found to be very robust and able to keep pace with change in the derivatives space.

---

[7] Major currencies are USD, EUR, JPY, GBP, CHF, CAD, SKR.

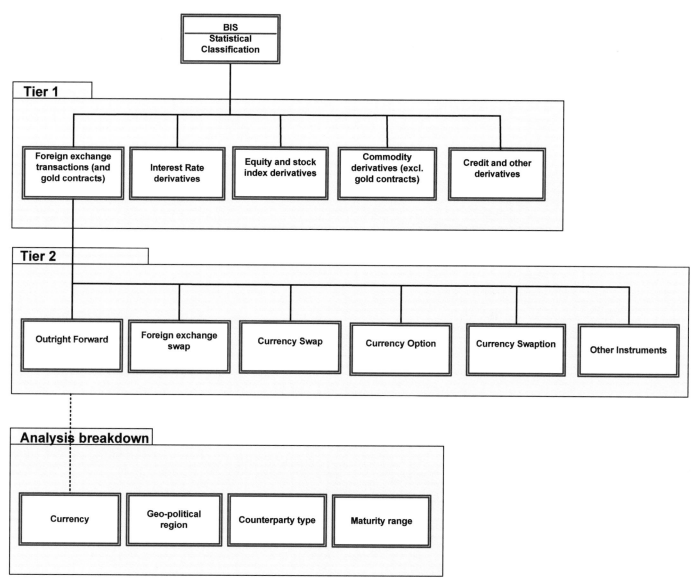

Figure 21. Snippet of the BIS - Derivative instruments classification scheme

Table 22B: Amounts outstanding of OTC equity-linked derivatives
By instrument and market
In billions of US dollars

Instrument / market	Notional amounts outstanding					Gross market values				
	Jun 2009	Dec 2009	Jun 2010	Dec 2010	Jun 2011	Jun 2009	Dec 2009	Jun 2010	Dec 2010	Jun 2011
Total contracts	**6,584**	**5,937**	**6,260**	**5,635**	**6,841**	**879**	**708**	**706**	**648**	**708**
US equities	1,512	1,749	1,732	1,565	1,739	202	192	195	191	202
European equities	3,883	3,167	3,227	2,793	3,414	478	373	352	311	342
Japanese equities	627	494	602	595	712	93	80	91	77	79
Other Asian equities	173	180	258	252	346	56	27	25	24	24
Latin American equities	125	38	105	58	77	8	5	6	5	7
Other equities	264	309	336	372	554	43	32	38	39	55
Forwards and swaps	**1,678**	**1,652**	**1,754**	**1,828**	**2,029**	**225**	**176**	**189**	**167**	**176**
US equities	520	528	571	544	551	55	46	63	51	48
European equities	915	877	899	941	1,016	130	105	99	91	92
Japanese equities	69	63	84	79	101	12	8	9	7	7
Other Asian equities	34	29	29	52	62	6	4	3	4	5
Latin American equities	34	20	17	20	42	5	3	3	2	4
Other equities	107	136	154	192	257	18	11	12	13	20
Options	**4,906**	**4,285**	**4,506**	**3,807**	**4,813**	**654**	**532**	**518**	**480**	**532**
US equities	992	1,221	1,161	1,022	1,188	147	146	132	140	155
European equities	2,968	2,290	2,328	1,852	2,398	348	268	253	220	249
Japanese equities	559	431	518	516	611	81	72	82	71	72
Other Asian equities	139	151	230	200	284	50	23	22	20	18
Latin American equities	90	19	88	37	35	3	2	3	3	3
Other equities	158	173	181	180	296	25	21	26	27	34

Figure 22. BIS – Triennial report of OTC equity-linked derivatives

Business context
The objective of this classification is to support the creation of the semi-annual derivatives markets statistics reports and the triennial central bank survey of foreign exchange and OTC derivatives market activity.

Online references
The majority of the material within this section has been extrapolated from BIS publications, including:

- Reporting guidelines for the turnover part of the triennial central bank survey of foreign exchange and OTC derivatives market activity in April 2010: www.bis.org/statistics/triennialrep/triennial_turnover_rd_repguid.pdf

- Guide to the international financial statistics: www.bis.org/statistics/intfinstatsguide.pdf

- For output based on classification, please refer to: www.bis.org/statistics/derstats.htm

Chapter 13

CFTC Regulatory reporting

13. CFTC regulatory reporting

The Commodity Futures Trading Commission (CFTC) defined the new rule titled, *"Real-Time Public Reporting of Swap Transaction Data; Final Rule (17 CFR Part 43)", that outlined the use of a* number of terms used for categorizing financial products to meet the requirements of the Dodd Frank Act. Nonetheless, the CFTC position paper published in February 2012 supports the use of a UPI.

The four terms identified in the *Final Rule* are *Asset class, sub-Asset class, Contract type* and *Contract sub-type.* Each term takes the form of a two alpha characters codification. An example given is Asset class="IR" and Contract type="S-". The code lists for the terms are not supplied within the Rule. Nonetheless, *Asset class* codes will exist for "Interest rate", "FX", "Credit", "Equity" and "Other commodity". Rule 17 *states* "Proposed § 43.2(e) provided that the asset classes include five major categories: Interest rate, FX[8], credit, equity and "other commodity[9], as well as any other asset class that may be

determined by the Commission.",…"The Commission is persuaded by the suggestions regarding the subdivision of asset classes and agrees that fewer asset classes will decrease fragmentation of data and reduce the burden of market participants to reconcile among multiple Swaps Data (trade) Repositories ("SDR"s)."

The *sub-Asset class* will contain an indication of a more specific description of the asset class. For example, with an *Asset class* of "Other commodity", the *sub-Asset class* will contain the code for "Energy", "Precious metals", "Metals-other", "Agriculture", "Weather", "Emissions" and "Volatility".

Contract type will include, but not limited to, "Swap", "Swaption" and "Standalone option". Similarly, *Contract sub-type* will provide a more specific indication of the product and for example, may include, but not limited to, "Basis swap", "Index swap", "Broad based security swap" and "Basket swap".

Business context
OTC derivatives record keeping and transaction reporting of deals that falls under the scope of the Dodd-Frank Act and within the responsibility of the CFTC.

Online references
CFTC 17 CFR Part 43 - Real-Time Public Reporting of Swap Transaction Data; Final Rule:

www.cftc.gov/ucm/groups/public/@lrfederalregister/documents/file/2011-33173a.pdf

CFTC Position Paper:
(http://www.cftc.gov/ucm/groups/public/@newsroom/documents/file/federalregister122011b.pdf

---

[8] the Commission agrees that clarification and additional guidance is needed to address FX products.103 Specifically, the Commission has determined to include cross-currency swaps in the interest rate asset class and FX options, swaps and forwards will be included in an FX asset class. Therefore, the Commission has modified the definition to better reflect the fact that the industry typically characterizes "currency" swaps as "interest rate swaps." 104 Accordingly, the Commission is replacing the term "currency" in the definition of asset class with "foreign exchange" in § 43.2 to accurately reflect the asset classes employed by the swaps market.

[9] the "other commodity" asset class remains an asset class that includes energy, metals, precious metals, agricultural commodities, weather, property and other commodities.

Chapter 14

FpML Product classification (Pre-2012)

14. FpML Product classification (Pre-2012)

Prior to 2012, FpML used the Asset class and the Product type code lists to provide the ability to classify OTC financial products.

By adding the product identifier in messages, this provided the user with the facility to support a unique product identification mechanism.

The Asset class code list:

Asset Class Short Name
Credit
InterestRate
ForeignExchange
Equity
Commodity

The Product type code list (version 1.4), comprises of 30 entries:

Product Type Short Name
AssetSwap
BondOption
BulletPayment
BullionForward
CapFloor
CommodityOption
CommoditySwap
ConvertibleBondOption
CreditDefaultBasket
CreditDefaultBasketTranche
CreditDefaultIndex
CreditDefaultIndexTranche
CreditDefaultOption
CreditDefaultSwap
CrossCurrencySwap
DividendSwap
EquityForward
EquityOption
FRA
FxForward
FxOption
FxOptionStrategy
FxSpot

FxSwap
InflationSwap
InterestRateSwap
InterestRateSwaption
TermDeposit
TotalReturnSwap
VarianceSwap

Business context

To classify and identify OTC derivative products between participants.

Online references

Product Type:
www.fpml.org/coding-scheme/product-type-simple-1-4.xml

Asset Class:
www.fpml.org/coding-scheme/asset-class

All FpML Code lists:
www.fpml.org/coding-scheme/

Chapter 15

FpML Product classification review (2011)

15. FpML Product classification review (2011)

The FpML reporting and regulatory reporting working group was reinstated in the spring of 2011 to assess the requirements of the Dodd-Frank Act and EMIR, primarily with the aim of identifying solutions to meet the real-time transparency and record keeping requirements of the regulations.

As part of this initiative it was acknowledged that the creation of an appropriate financial product typology would be essential. To that end, an investigation into the OTC classifications used elsewhere in the market was undertaken. This resulted in the creation of the OTC classifications matrix. This work was a useful exercise as it formed that basis of the FpML 2011 classification proposal as well as identifying the FpML development roadmap.

C	J	K	L	N	O	Y
	MiFID	CFTC 17	CFTC 17	BANK OF INTERNATIONAL SETTLEMENTS Tier 1	Teir 2	
Product	Derviative Type	Asset Class & Sub-asset Classs	Contract type			Description
Asset Swap	Swaps (other than CfDs, TRS and CDS) (S)	Interest rate ("IR")	swap ("S?")	Single-currency interest rate derivatives	Interest rate swap	An interest rate swap whose fixed stream mimics the coupons of a specified asset, typically a bond security.
Cancelable IRS	Swaps (S)	Interest rate ("IR")	swap ("S?")	Single-currency interest rate derivatives	Interest rate swap?	An interest rate swap for which one of the parties has the right but not the obligation to cancel remaining cashflows at one or more dates during the term of the swap.
Cash Payment	Not within scope of MiFID	Not within scope CFTC	Not within scope CFTC	Not within scope BIS?	Not within scope BIS?	A single payment of a fixed cash amount on a specified date.
Cross-currency swap	Not within scope of MiFID	Currency ("CU")	swap ("S?")	FX transactions	Currency Swap	Contract which commits two counterparties to exchange streams of interest payments in different currencies for an agreed period of time and to exchange principal amounts in different currencies at a pre-agreed exchange rate at maturity.
Currency swaption	Not within scope of MiFID	Currency ("CU")	Swaption ("SO")	FX transactions	Currency swaption	OTC option to enter into a cross-currency swap contract.

Figure 23. Snippet of OTC Classifications Matrix

Classification proposal (2011)

The matrix, a snapshot is provided above, was later supplemented with a classification scheme recommendation comprising of an *Asset class,* construct, along with the recommendation to simply of the product type code list, such that it contains purely, "Base product" entries. This material was subsequently provided to the various ISDA asset class working groups (Credit, Equities, Commodities, etc...) to construct their respective taxonomies. These taxonomies form an essential component of the ISDA Unique Product Identifier (UPI) initiative.

ISDA website category	FpML 1.0 code	Proposed Code	Sub-asset Class	Product Category	Examples
Credit Derivatives / Credit Default Swaps					
	Credit	Credit			
		Credit	(Corporate Bond/Credit Bond/Debt)		
		Credit	Debt	Single Name	Single name CDS, credit bond return swap
		Credit	Debt	Index	index CDS
		Credit	Debt	Basket	basket CDS
		Credit	Loan	Loan	CDS on loan, loan index
		Credit	Mortgage	Mortgage	CDS on mortgage, mortgage index
Equity Derivatives					
	Equities	Equity			
		Equity	Common equity (stocks)		
		Equity	Equity	Price return	Equity price return swap
		Equity	Equity	Dividend return	dividend swap
		Equity	Equity	Total return	Equity total return swap
		Equity	Equity	Variance/volatility	variance swap
		Equity	Mutual funds (just an equity?)	Mutual funds (just an equity?)	
		Equity	Convertible bonds	Convertible bonds	OTC convertible bond option
Interest Rates Derivatives					
	InterestRates	InterestRate			
		InterestRate	Single-currency rates	Single-currency rates	
		InterestRate	SingleCurrency	fixed-float	vanilla fixed-float IR swap
		InterestRate	SingleCurrency	float-float, basis	basis swap, e.g. prime vs libor
		InterestRate	SingleCurrency	specialized indexes/swap types	CMS, CMT
		InterestRate	CrossCurrency	CrossCurrency	cross currency swap, cross currency swaption
		InterestRate	Inflation	Inflation	inflation swap
FX Derivatives					
	ForeignExchange	ForeignExchange			
		ForeignExchange	G10 Currencies		spot, forward, swap, option on USD, EUR, JPY

Figure 24. Snippet of FpML proposal based on the findings of Classifications Matrix

The FpML OTC classification proposal (a snippet is shown in Figure 24) comprises four terms, ISDA website category (or Asset class), sub-Asset class, Product category as above and Product type which is not shown in the figure above.

The FpML Product classification review, which led to the FpML classification proposal, both of which were primarily the joint brainchild of Martin Sexton (London Market Systems) and Brian Lynn (Global Electronic Markets, Inc.).

Asset class hierarchy

The Asset class code list can be supplemented with the *sub-Asset class* and *Product category* terms to allow users to drilldown to identify specific product types. An example classification is: Asset class = "Commodities", sub-Asset = "Energy" and Product category = "Gas".

Asset class
Credit
InterestRates
ForeignExchange
Equities
Commodities
Structured Products and others (Hybrids)

57

sub-Asset

The entries in this term are Asset class specific.

Product category

The entries in this term are Asset class/sub-Asset class specific.

Product type

The proposal was to cleanse/simplify the product type code list so that it no longer contained explicit contract types (e.g. Variance Swap). The proposal limited the entries to Base products and included the following entries:

Product type
Swap
Forward
Option
Swaption
Warrant

Business context

The classification of OTC Derivative instruments to support the mandated requirements of Dodd-Frank and EMIR for real-time transparency and Record keeping purposes.

Chapter 16

ISDA Unique Product Identifier

16. ISDA Unique Product Identifier

The aim of the development of the ISDA Unique Product Identifier (UPI) is to support the identification requirements of all the participants involved in the reporting of OTC derivative products. The types of participants include Swap Execution Facilities (SEFs), Central Counterparty Clearing Houses (CCPs), Swap Data Repositories (SDRs) and other key market players.

In addition, to the unique identification of the product dealt, the UPI also requires the allocation of the appropriate classification. This is achieved by using one the appropriate Asset class taxonomies. These asset classes include Credit, Interest Rates, Equities, FX and Commodities. Each taxonomy was developed in isolation by subject matter experts. All were provided with the same single inheritance hierarchy:

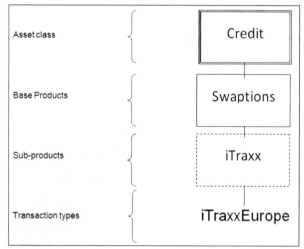

Figure 25. ISDA's Taxonomies Scheme

The hierarchy under each asset class comprises of three related terms, namely Base product, sub-Product and Transaction type. A further extension to this scheme is provided for commodities to support the *Settlement type* (this can have the value "cash" or "physical delivery").

FpML Product taxonomy code list

A spreadsheet of the taxonomies has been published by ISDA, this information is used to create an FpML product taxonomy code list equivalent. Each entry in the code list takes the form of a Uniform Resource Name (URN), an identifier where each term is separated by a colon. Similar to an ISBN construct, an example of the FpML product taxonomy entry is:

Commodity:Metals:Precious:SpotFwd:Physical

FpML Product Taxonomies code list

The latest version of the Product taxonomy code list can be found at:

www.fpml.org/coding-scheme/product-taxonomy

Business context

The ISDA taxonomies/UPI combination is designed to support the regulatory requirements of Dodd-Frank and EMIR which both focus on increased transparency for public and regulatory reporting.

Online references

ISDA Identifiers and OTC Taxonomies:
www2.isda.org/otc-taxonomies-and-upi/

Chapter 17

ESMA MiFID Derivative Type

17. ESMA MiFID Derivative Type

The Derivative Type term forms part of the Alternative Instrument Identifier (AII)[10] and is used to classify derivative instruments that falls under the remit of the Markets in Financial Instruments Directive (MiFiD). The ESMA Derivative Type is a code list which comprises the following values:

O = Option
W = Warrant
F = Future
D = Contract for Difference (CfD) and Total Return Swap (TRS)
X = Spread bet
S = Swap, excluding CfD, TRS and CDS
Z = Credit Default Swap (CDS)
K = Complex derivative product

Some regulators have found this code list insufficient to meet their needs, and in the case of the FSA, they have extended this list to include:

Q = Spreadbet on an option on an equity
Y = Contract for difference on an option on an equity

Business context

Transaction and trade reporting requirements under MiFID, the European Union law that provides harmonized regulation for investment services across the 30 member states of the European Economic Area (the 27 Member States of the European Union plus Iceland, Norway and Liechtenstein).

Online references

AII Definition:
www.londonmarketsystems.com/AII/

---

[10] A symbolic identifier used to uniquely identify derivative products comprising 7 terms (Venue Identification, Exchange Code, Strike Price, Currency Code, Delivery Date, Call/Put Indicator and Derivative Type).

Chapter 18

Accountancy Standards

18. Accountancy Standards

All of the accountancy standards (IAS 32, IAS 39, IFRS 7, and IFRS 9) are principles based and neither the International Accounting Standards (IAS) nor the International Financial Reporting Standards (IFRS) publish a classification scheme per se. Nonetheless there is common approach to ledger entries and groupings of entries, and not surprisingly the ledger codes are grouped by asset class and then by product type.

The primary reason for classifying financial products in this domain is to be able to recognise and measure financial assets and liabilities.

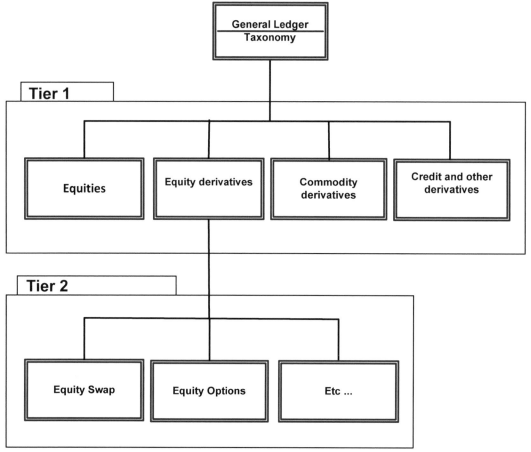

Figure 26. General Ledger classification

This can also take the form of a Dewey decimal classification scheme, as provided in "*Chapter 2. How are classifications constructed?*", please refer to Figure 4 for an example of this.

Business context

To summarise each standard:

IAS 32 — Financial Instruments covers the presenting financial information,

IAS 39 and its replacement IFRS 9 defines the requirements for recognition and measurement (financial assets and liabilities) of financial products, and

IFRS 7 Financial Instruments: Disclosures.

Chapter 19

RIXML Product Classification

19. RIXML Product Classification

Uses a simple set of code lists for categorising products in publications, namely AssetClass, AssetType and SecurityType which are all discretionary within the ProductClassifications container. This container also includes geo-political information, index/fund information as well as the ability to group by industry sector by means of a freeform textual description. It is worth highlighting that there is no logic applied or relationship between these terms and all are optional in the XML document.

Asset Class
Equity
FixedIncome
Currency
Commodities

Asset Type
Stock
Convertible
USTreasuries
SovereignCredit
AgencyCredit
MoneyMarketCredit
CorporateInvestmentGradeCredit
CorporateHighYieldCredit
MortgageBackedCredit
MunicipalCredit
AssetBackedCredit
EmergingMarketsSovereign
EmergingMarketsCredit
SupranationalCredit
CollateralizedDebtObligations
Credit
Loans
EuropeanCoveredBond
Derivatives
FinancialFutures
EquityFunds
BondFunds
MoneyMarketFunds
BalancedFunds
CurrencyCash
CurrencyDerivatives
CurrencyFutures
CommodityFunds
PublisherDefined

Security Type
Bonds
DiscountNotesAndBills
FixedRateNotes
FloatingRateNotes
MediumTermNotes
CommercialPaper
BankerAcceptances
Deposits
EuroBonds
EuroDenominatedNotes
InflationLinkedBonds
Strips
Repo
SamuraiNotes
YankeeNotes
ConvertiblePreferred
ConvertibleStructured
Warrants
Futures
Swaps
Options
Swaptions
StructuredNotes
PrivatePlacements144A
Preferred
ADR/GDR
ClosedEndFund
OpenEndFund
Gold
Silver
Aluminum
Platinum
Copper
Wheat
Corn
Coffee
Cocoa
Cotton
…

Business context

The distribution of decision making material (i.e. investment research).

Online references

RIXML datatypes Schema:
www.rixml.org/newsite/specifications/v2
31/RIXML-datatypes-2_3_1.xsd

66

Chapter 20

EDM Council's
Semantic Repository

20. EDM Council's Semantic Repository

The Council's Semantic Repository gets a mention in this publication as the rules for creation of any classification should be based on a semantic analysis, which requires a good appreciation of the underlying Characteristics of financial products.

The real challenge for an organisation is transforming a conceptual semantic model into an operational equivalent and even after transformation, a complex poly-hierarchical structure can result in a complex model making the extraction of key information into a classification difficult to achieve. Therefore a mechanism would need to be developed to create a classification scheme that can be used in an operational environment. The EDM Council has initiated an operational OTC Semantic proof of concept that is examining ways of representing this information and identifying the key features of vanilla IRS products. For further information about the proof of concept, please refer to the section titled, "Semantic Metadata approach" in Chapter 21 - Modelling Classifications".

The sample below, based on the snapshot of the Semantic Repository, shows the different paths in the model hierarchy that a product may take and the associated classification term that can be applied.

Level 1	Level 2	Level 3	Level 4	Level 5	Level 6	Level 7	Level 8	Feature
Financial Instrument	Contract	Derivative Contract						
			Swap Contract					Base produc
				Interest Rate				Asset class
					Basis Swap Contract			sub-Produc
Financial Instrument	Contract	Bilateral Contract	Economic Contract	OTC Instrument				
					Swap Contract			Base produc
						Interest Rate		Asset class
							Basis Swap Contract	sub-Produc

Figure 27. Semantic Model: Deep poly hierarchical example

Chapter 21

Solvency II: Complementary Identification Code (CIC)

21. Solvency II: Complementary Identification Code (CIC)

The Solvency II Directive 2009/138/EC is an EU Directive that codifies and harmonises the EU insurance regulation. This directive asks a number of questions from organisations regarding the common use of identifiers for assets and counterparty, as well as the need for the classification of assets.

The associated classification scheme is known as the Complementary Identification Code (CIC) and its aim is to combine a product's characteristics and risk exposure and thus allow supervisors to perform different aggregations and analyses by classes of securities.

The CIC structure

The European Insurance and Occupational Pensions Authority (EIOPA) created the CIC, which is a codification based on a four Alpha/numeric character string. It has a hierarchical structure comprising the country code of Listing, ISO 3166-1-alpha-2 country code or XL (for not listed) or XT (for not exchange tradable), followed by one character used to identify the financial Base Product (referred to as an asset by EIOPA) grouping, and the fourth character the explicit product type.

CIC example

Equity rights can be represented using the code, "GB33"[11]. This is broken down as follows:

Country of Listing	Base product (Asset)	Product (Asset) type
GB (United Kingdom)	3 (Equity)	3 (Equity rights)

The use of the country code does result in some confusion. It is not strictly clear when the country code XL (for non listed assets) should be used instead of XT (for non traded assets) and one could question why jurisdiction of the contract is not captured rather than the country code as the two are not always synonymous.

Like other attempts to classify financial products, there is the possibility of overlapping Product types as well as mutually exclusivity, with a product being mapped onto a different code, based on its use.

---

[11] Also, see the CIC table on page 74, which shows the "Equity rights", shaded in the table.

The Base (Asset) product groups are:

Code	Description
1	Government bonds
2	Corporate bonds
3	Equity
4	Investment funds
5	Structured notes
6	Collateralised securities
7	Cash and equivalents
8	Mortgages and loans
9	Property
A	Futures
B	Call Options
C	Put Options
D	Swaps
E	Forwards
F	Credit derivatives

Subsequently products are then broken down into sub-categories (or product types) and thus the following table can be constructed. This and further information on this subject can be obtained at http://eiopa.europa.eu/

Category (Position 3)	1	2	3	4	5	6	7	8
	Government bonds	Corporate bonds	Equity	Investment funds	Structured notes	Collateralised securities	Cash and equivalents	Mortgages and loans
Sub-category or main risk (Position 4)	11	21	31	41	51	61	71	81
	Central Government bonds	Common bonds	Common equity	Equity funds	Equity risk	Equity risk	Cash	Uncollateralized loans made
	12	22	32	42	52	62	72	82
	Supra-national bonds	Convertible bonds	Equity of real estate related corporation	Debt funds	Interest rate risk	Interest rate risk	Transferable deposits	Loans made collateralized with securities
	13	23	33	43	53	63	73	
	Regional government bonds	Commercial paper	Equity rights	Money market funds	Currency risk	Currency risk	Other deposits short term (less than one year)	
	14	24	34	44	54	64	74	84
	Municipal government bonds	Money market instruments	Preferred equity	Asset allocation funds	Credit risk	Credit risk	Other deposits with term longer than one year	Mortgages
	15	25		45	55	65	75	85
	Treasury bonds	Hybrid bonds		Real estate funds	Real estate risk	Real estate risk	Cash deposits to cedants	Other collateralized loans made
	16	26		46	56	66		
	Covered bond	Covered bond		Alternative funds	Commodity risk	Commodity risk		
				47	57	67		
				Commodity funds	Catastrophe and Weather risk	Catastrophe and Weather risk		
				48	58	68		
				Infrastructure funds	Mortality risk	Mortality risk		
	19	29	39	49	59	69	79	89
	Other	Other	Other	Other	Other	Other	Other	Other

Figure 28. Complementary Identification Code (CIC) classification table (Part 1 of 2)

Category	9	A	B	C	D	E	F
	Property	Futures	Call Options	Put Options	Swaps	Forwards	Credit derivatives
Sub-category or main risk	91	1	1	1	1	1	1
	Property (office and commercial)	Equity and index futures	Equity and index options	Equity and index options	Interest rate swaps	FRA	Credit default swap
	92	2	2	2	2	2	2
	Property (residential)	Interest rate futures	Bond options	Bond options	Currency swaps	FRA	Credit spread option
	93	3	3	3	3		3
	Property (for own use)	Currency futures	Currency options	Currency options	Interest rate and currency swaps		Credit spread swap
	94						4
	Property (under construction)						Total return swap
	95	5	5	5	5		
	Plant and equipment (for own use)	Commodity futures	Commodity options	Commodity options	Security swaps		
			6	6			
			Swaptions	Swaptions			
			7	7			
			Warrants	Warrants			
	99						
	Other						

Figure 29. Complementary Identification Code (CIC) classification table (Part 2 of 2)

This page has been intentionally left blank.

Chapter 22

AIFMD: Asset type typology

22. AIFMD: Asset type typology

The Alternative Investment Fund Managers Directive (AIFMD) 2011/61/EU is a European Union Directive that regulates fund managers that manage primarily hedge funds and private equity funds.

The Directive is very prescriptive and requires the reporting entities to codify funds and assets within based an exposure asset type typology.

The Asset type typology structure

The typology is based on a hierarchical structure, three deep. Each level uses a 3/4 character abbreviation to identify the Macro Asset type, the asset type and sub-asset type. In the XML reporting message it may contain the codification at the highest level, e.g. SEC, however primary assets can be represented at the Sub Asset Type level which means that the codification becomes a concatenation of the three features separated by an underscore ("_").

AIFMD Asset type typology example

Certificate of Deposit (CD) can be represented using the code, "SEC_CSH_CODP.

This is broken down as follows:

Macro Asset Type	Asset Type	Sub Asset Type
SEC (Securities)	SEC_CSH (Cash)	SEC_CSH_CODP (Certificate of Deposit)

Macro asset type

The possible values for the Macro Asset Type are:

Code	Description
SEC	Securities
DER	Derivatives
CIU	Collective Investment unit
PHY	Physical
OTH	Other assets
NTA	No assets to report

Asset type

The possible values for the Asset Type are:

Code	Description
SEC_CSH	Cash and cash equivalent
SEC_LEQ	Listed equities
SEC_UEQ	Unlisted equities
SEC_CPN	Corporate bonds not issued by financial institutions
SEC_CPI	Corporate bonds issued by financial institutions
SEC_SBD	Sovereign bonds

EC_MBN	Municipal bonds
SEC_CBN	Convertible bonds not issued by financial institutions
SEC_CBI	Convertible bonds issued by financial institutions
SEC_LON	Loans
SEC_SSP	Structured/securitised products
DER_EQD	Equity derivatives
DER_FID	Fixed income derivatives
DER_CDS	CDS
DER_FEX	Foreign exchange
DER_IRD	Interest rate derivatives
DER_CTY	Commodity derivatives
DER_OTH	Other derivatives
PHY_RES	Physical: real estate
PHY_CTY	Physical: Commodities
PHY_TIM	Physical: Timber
PHY_ART	Physical: Art and collectables
PHY_TPT	Physical: Transportation assets
PHY_OTH	Physical: Other
CIU_OAM	Investment in CIU operated/managed by the AIFM
CIU_NAM	Investment in CIU not operated/managed by the AIFM
OTH_OTH	Total Other
NTA_NTA	N/A

Sub Asset Type

The possible values for the Sub Asset Type are:

Code	Description
SEC_CSH_CODP	Certificates of deposit
SEC_CSH_COMP	Commercial papers
SEC_CSH_OTHD	Other deposits
SEC_CSH_OTHC	Other cash and cash equivalents (excluding government securities)
SEC_LEQ_IFIN	Listed equities issued by financial institutions
SEC_LEQ_OTHR	Other listed equity
SEC_UEQ_UEQY	Unlisted equities
SEC_CPN_INVG	Corporate bonds not issued by financial institutions-Investment grade
SEC_CPN_NIVG	Corporate bonds not issued by financial institutions-Non-investment grade
SEC_CPI_INVG	Corporate bonds issued by financial institutions-Investment grade
SEC_CPI_NIVG	Corporate bonds issued by financial institutions-Non-investment grade
SEC_SBD_EUBY	EU bonds with a 0-1 year term to maturity
SEC_SBD_EUBM	EU bonds with a 1+ year term to maturity
SEC_SBD_NOGY	Non-G10 bonds with a 0-1 year term to maturity
SEC_SBD_NOGM	Non-G10 bonds with a 1+ year term to maturity

SEC_SBD_EUGY	G10 non EU bonds with a 0-1 year term to maturity
SEC_SBD_EUGM	G10 non EU bonds with a 1+ year term to maturity
SEC_MBN_MNPL	Municipal bonds
SEC_CBN_INVG	Convertible bonds not issued by financial institutions-Investment grade
SEC_CBN_NIVG	Convertible bonds not issued by financial institutions Non-investment grade
SEC_CBI_INVG	Convertible bonds issued by financial institutions Investment grade
SEC_CBI_NIVG	Convertible bonds issued by financial institutions-Non-investment grade
SEC_LON_LEVL	Leveraged loans
SEC_LON_OTHL	Other loans
SEC_SSP_SABS	ABS
SEC_SSP_RMBS	RMBS
SEC_SSP_CMBS	CMBS
SEC_SSP_AMBS	Agency MBS
SEC_SSP_ABCP	ABCP
SEC_SSP_CDOC	CDO/CLO
SEC_SSP_STRC	Structured certificates
SEC_SSP_SETP	ETP
SEC_SSP_OTHS	Other Structured/securitised products
DER_EQD_FINI	Equity derivatives related to financial institutions
DER_EQD_OTHD	Other equity derivatives
DER_FID_FIXI	Fixed income derivatives
DER_CDS_SNFI	Single name financial CDS
DER_CDS_SNSO	Single name sovereign CDS
DER_CDS_SNOT	Single name other CDS
DER_CDS_INDX	Index CDS
DER_CDS_EXOT	Exotic (incl. credit default tranche)
DER_CDS_OTHR	Other CDS
DER_FEX_INVT	Foreign exchange (for investment purposes)
DER_FEX_HEDG	Foreign exchange (for hedging purposes)
DER_IRD_INTR	Interest rate derivatives
DER_CTY_ECOL	Energy/Crude oil
DER_CTY_ENNG	Energy/Natural gas
DER_CTY_ENPW	Energy/Power
DER_CTY_ENOT	Energy/Other
DER_CTY_PMGD	Precious metals/Gold
DER_CTY_PMOT	Precious metals/Other
DER_CTY_OTIM	Other commodities/Industrial metals
DER_CTY_OTLS	Other commodities/Livestock
DER_CTY_OTAP	Other commodities/Agricultural products
DER_CTY_OTHR	Other commodities/Other
DER_OTH_OTHR	Other derivatives

PHY_RES_RESL	Residential real estate
PHY_RES_COML	Commercial real estate
PHY_RES_OTHR	Other real estate
PHY_CTY_PCTY	Physical: Commodities
PHY_TIM_PTIM	Physical: Timber
PHY_ART_PART	Physical: Art and collectables
PHY_TPT_PTPT	Physical: Transportation assets
PHY_OTH_OTHR	Physical: Other
CIU_OAM_MMFC	Investment in CIU operated/managed by the AIFM-Money Market Funds and cash management CIU
CIU_OAM_AETF	Investment in CIU operated/managed by the AIFM-ETF
CIU_OAM_OTHR	Investment in CIU operated/managed by the AIFM-Other CIU
CIU_NAM_MMFC	Investment in CIU not operated/managed by the AIFM-Money Market Funds and cash management CIU
CIU_NAM_AETF	Investment in CIU not operated/managed by the AIFM-ETF
CIU_NAM_OTHR	Investment in CIU not operated/managed by the AIFM-Other CIU
OTH_OTH_OTHR	Total Other
NTA_NTA_NOTA	N/A

The above code-lists are based on the XSD schemas published by ESMA. The AIFMD reporting guidelines contains further information regarding the use of the classification.

Annex VII: Table of enumerated reporting fields values

Table 1 - Asset type typology for all exposures reporting (excluding turnover):

Macro asset type		Asset type		Sub-asset type	
Code	Label	Code	Label	Code	Label
SEC	Securities	SEC_CSH	Cash and cash equivalent	SEC_CSH_CODP	Certificates of deposit
SEC	Securities	SEC_CSH	Cash and cash equivalent	SEC_CSH_COMP	Commercial papers
SEC	Securities	SEC_CSH	Cash and cash equivalent	SEC_CSH_OTHD	Other deposits
SEC	Securities	SEC_CSH	Cash and cash equivalent	SEC_CSH_OTHC	Other cash and cash equivalents (excluding government securities)
SEC	Securities	SEC_LEQ	Listed equities	SEC_LEQ_IFIN	Listed equities issued by financial institutions
SEC	Securities	SEC_LEQ	Listed equities	SEC_LEQ_OTHR	Other listed equity
SEC	Securities	SEC_UEQ	Unlisted equities	SEC_UEQ_UEQY	Unlisted equities
SEC	Securities	SEC_CBN	Corporate bonds not issued by financial institutions	SEC_CBN_INVG	Corporate bonds not issued by financial institutions-Investment grade
SEC	Securities	SEC_CBN	Corporate bonds not issued by financial institutions	SEC_CBN_NIVG	Corporate bonds not issued by financial institutions-Non-investment grade
SEC	Securities	SEC_CBI	Corporate bonds issued by financial institutions	SEC_CBI_INVG	Corporate bonds issued by financial institutions-Investment grade

Business context
Regulatory reporting by fund managers of primarily hedge funds and private equity fund.

Online references

AIFMD Reporting Guidelines:
http://www.esma.europa.eu/system/files/2013-592_consultation_paper_on_esma_guidelines_on_aifmd_reporting_for_publication.pdf

Chapter 23

Harmonisation of the Unique Product Identifier

23. Harmonisation of the Unique Product Identifier

This classification scheme was proposed by the Committee on Payments and Market Infrastructures, Board of the International Organization of Securities Commissions (BIOSC), in the form of a Consultative report for the "Harmonisation of the Unique Product Identifier (UPI)" , published Dec 2015.

The proposal is based on a hierarchical structure of 3 instrument types, comprising ("Forward, Swap and Option") or uber contract styles, under which all other contract styles need to fit into. This is rather ambitious. Consider a Swaption or a Loan contract, which if any, of the proposed instrument types should these agreement reside?

The report states, " To structure the discussion of the UPI and what it should cover, the following concepts are useful: instrument type, product, contract and transaction. Their relationships are illustrated in the following diagram:"

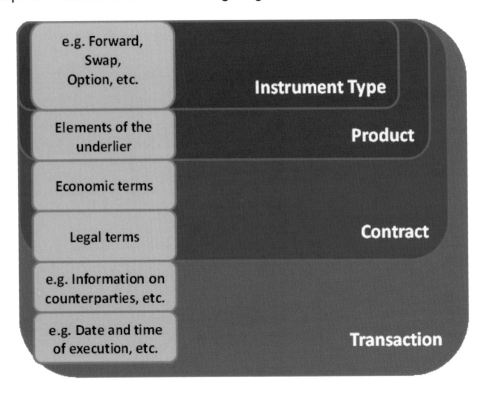

Figure 30. Harmonisation of Unique Product Identifier[12]

---

[12] Taken from proposal: https://www.iosco.org/library/pubdocs/pdf/IOSCOPD519.pdf

When one normalises this structure, the hierarchy can be broken down into the following model:

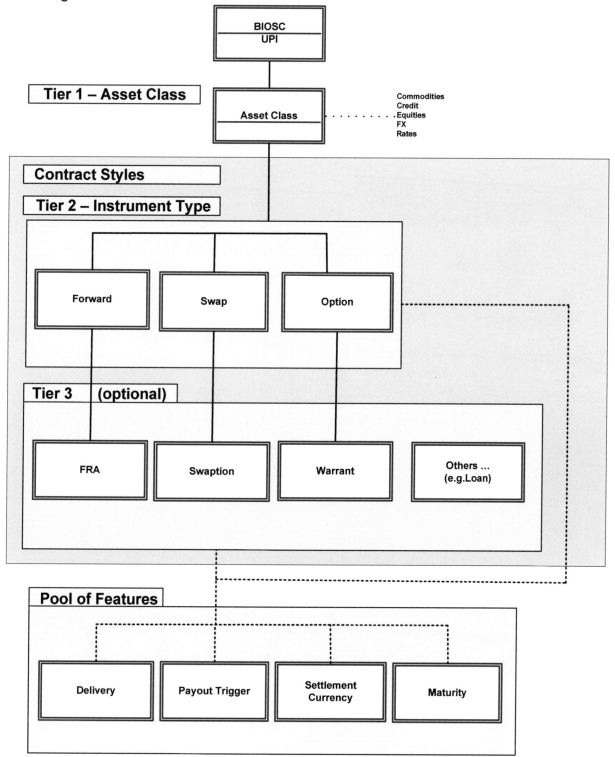

Figure 31. Harmonisation of Unique Product Identifier Scheme Hierarchy

Business context

The report states, " The Aggregation Feasibility Study calls for "the standardisation of the depiction of financial products/instruments/contracts across markets and geographies" for the purpose of data aggregation.

Online Reference:

https://www.iosco.org/library/pubdocs/pdf/IOSCOPD519.pdf

Chapter 24

Modelling Classifications

24. Modelling Classifications

There are various ways of representing classifications. It is possible to present a classification scheme in a tabular form, such as a spreadsheet, assuming that one is dealing with a strict hierarchical structure with only a small number of features to capture and one or two similar use cases. Beyond this however, the limitations of a spreadsheet become apparent.

Each business process/application may wish to classify in a different way depending on the components that make up the product and the business context. The common example used is the classification of a convertible instrument which is traded as an Equity product but has debt components. For P&L calculations and default scenarios relating to the issuer the debt components override the Equity product type. A spreadsheet is definitely not appropriate, so what is?

Of course, XML can provide the framework to represent a classification and likewise, Unified Modelling Language (UML) can also use a semantic Metadata approach using one of the two principal syntaxes, RDFS or OWL. Classifications can also be creating directly using ontology editing tools assuming an appropriate modelling methodology can be identified.

Modelling considerations using XML

XML does lend itself to modelling financial data, though it is primarily used for messaging. It has the capability to support enumerated code lists as well as "and", "or" and "exclusive or" relationships. It is important to ensure that the existing data architecture policies are taken into consideration when developing a classification scheme.

OASIS Genericode – Structured code list variant

I have used the OASIS Genericode standard to support ISO 10962 and other hierarchical structured code lists. The mechanism I deployed was to use a parent reference *(parentElement* in the column definitions*)* on each entry to support the hierarchical relationships and I also added a column to support versioning, vendor/user variants or if one wants multiple views (RE: *scheme*), as seen in the Figure below:

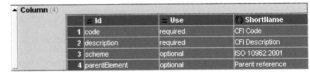

Column (4)			
	Id	Use	ShortName
1	code	required	CFI Code
2	description	required	CFI Description
3	scheme	optional	ISO 10962:2001
4	parentElement	optional	Parent reference

Figure 32. OASIS Genericode "Structured code list variant column definitions

Nonetheless, Anthony Coates, who defined the OASIS standard, would stress that Genericode was not designed to support structured code lists but merely simple code lists, though the user may wish to embed intelligence within the entries.

FpML Genericode representation of the ISDA Taxonomies

An alternative solution is to use Genericode and populate each entry in the form of an URI (e.g. InterestRate:IRSwap:FixedFloat), as adopted in FpML for the ISDA Taxonomies. The URI is used in the semantic world, hence its adoption in this context. Please refer to the following Genericode equivalent of the ISDA Taxonomies (the latest version): www.fpml.org/coding-scheme/product-taxonomy

Versioning is managed by adding a version number to the XML document: product-taxonomy-1-0.xml product-taxonomy-1-1.xml ...

SDMX Standard

Some in the industry have shown interest in using the SDMX standard for representing product classifications. This is because it provides the capability to support hierarchical structures, code lists and hierarchical dependencies within code lists themselves. An added advantage is that the governance process for versioning and maintenance of the Metadata is also part of the standard. "The Statistical Data and Metadata Exchange (SDMX) initiative (www.sdmx.org) conceived in 2001 sets standards that can facilitate the exchange of statistical data and Metadata using modern information technology, with an emphasis on aggregated data"[13].

This standard differentiates between the context in which the data exists (the Metadata) and the data itself. SDMX is an ISO standard (ISO/TS 17369:2005)

and is designed such that hierarchical structures can be represented within the Metadata component. Nonetheless, given that it has been primarily designed for the dissemination of time series data sets it is not necessarily appropriate for use in supporting financial product classifications. This is emphasised by the inclusion of the mandatory data item, *"PrimaryMeasureType"* which is required to allow consumers to easily identify the time dimension in any resulting XML documents.

SDMX code list documents can be defined by using the schema SDMXStructure.xsd and a snippet of an example follows.

```
<structure:Structures xmlns:structure="http://www.sdm
    xmlns:xsi="http://www.w3.org/2001/XMLSchema-i
    SDMXStructure.xsd">
    <!-- Add Hierachical code list to support catgory/g
    -->
- <structure:Codelists>
    <!-- ISO 10962 Categories code list -->
  - <structure:Codelist agencyID="ANNA" id="Category">
      <common:Name xmlns:common="http://www.sdm
    - <structure:Code id="D">
        <common:Name xmlns:common="http://www.sd
      </structure:Code>
    - <structure:Code id="E">
        <common:Name xmlns:common="http://www.sd
      </structure:Code>
    - <structure:Code id="R">
        <common:Name xmlns:common="http://www.sd
        </common:Name>
      </structure:Code>
    - <structure:Code id="O">
        <common:Name xmlns:common="http://www.sd
      </structure:Code>
    - <structure:Code id="F">
        <common:Name xmlns:common="http://www.sd
      </structure:Code>
    - <structure:Code id="M">
        <common:Name xmlns:common="http://www.sd
```

Figure 33. SDMX Code list sample of the ISO CFI Category

---

[13] SDMX Standards: Section 1 - Framework for SDMX Technical Standards - Version 2.1 April 2011

Modelling considerations using UML

Like XML, UML is a useful canvas on which to develop a classification scheme. The user has to consider the most appropriate mechanisms for supporting the hierarchical structure, the mutual exclusivity requirements and the enumerated code lists.

UML Class Model Solution

The simplest solution is to use the UML class model with the {xor} constraint to associate classes to support mutual exclusivity. An example of this can be seen in Figure 29 that shows a snippet of the ISO 10962 CFI where the constraint is applied to the Group classes under the "Equities" Category.

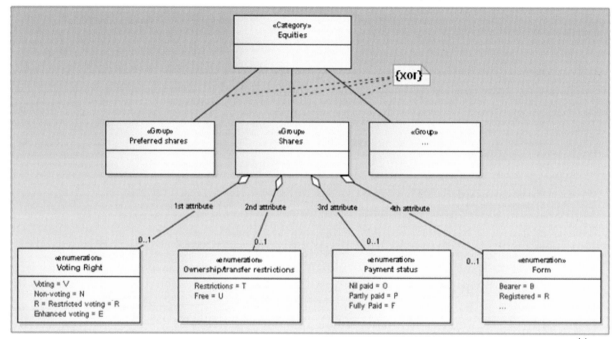

Figure 34 UML Class Model Representation of ISO CFI (Equities Category snippet)[14]

---

[14] Created using Sparx Systems Enterprise Architect

88

UML Generalization Set Solution

An alternative to a simple class model solution is to deploy the generalization set concept introduced in UML 2.0. The example model that follows highlights the important Characteristics associated with Option products.

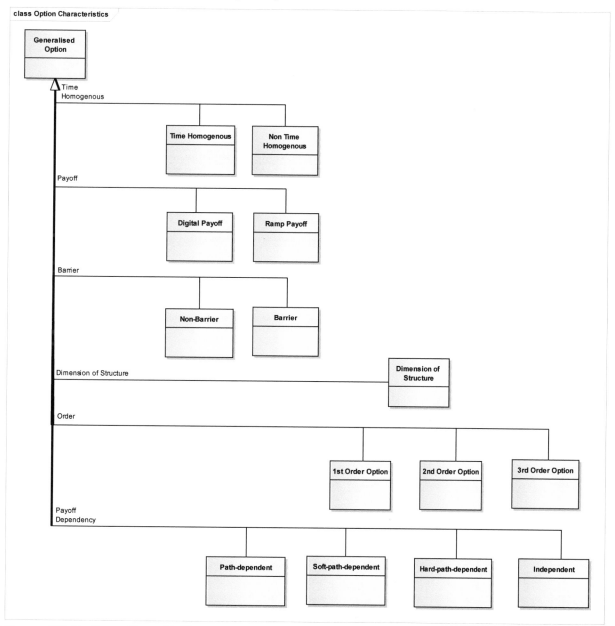

Figure 35 Options Payoff Characteristics based on UML Generalization Set concept

Nassim Taleb in the publication "Dynamic Hedging" identifies six dimensions of analysis important to understanding and pricing generalised options, these being:

Time Homogenous or Non Time Homogenous: An option where the contracted payoff structure does not change over the life of the instrument is known as Time Homogenous.

89

Digital or ramped payoff: A digital payoff (all or nothing) based on an event, whereas a ramp payoff is continuous between points.

Barrier(s) or non Barrier(s): The payoff structure changes when a price trigger point is hit (A barrier option).

Dimension of Structure The number of variables or assets. For example, a vanilla option has two dimensions, the asset price and time.

Order of Option: The first order is an option of an underlyer, an option of another is second order. An option on a second order option is a third order option.

Path Dependent: An Independent-path option has a payoff based on a specific event on expiry, whilst dependent-path options are based on one or more pieces of information. A memoryless-path is a single piece of information, such as a barrier trigger of an underlyer's price, whereas Hard-path-dependent is based on more than one piece of information.

ISO 20022 Modelling methodology

As a final example of the flexibility of UML, modelling financial product classifications using the ISO 20022 methodology is examined. As with the other modelling approaches, code lists and mutual exclusivity can be support, as well as the ability to generate the ISO 20022 XML message model components, used for data dissemination.

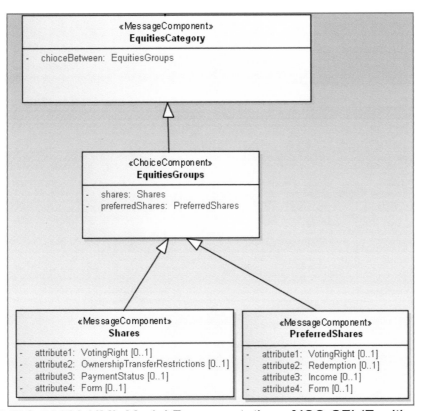

Figure 36 ISO 20022 UML Model Representation of ISO CFI (Equities snippet)

The ISO 20022 UML model in Figure 31, when run through an ISO 20022 message generator results in the creation of the XML equivalent (Figure 32). Please note that the ISO 20022 XML abbreviations have not been applied in the sample shown:

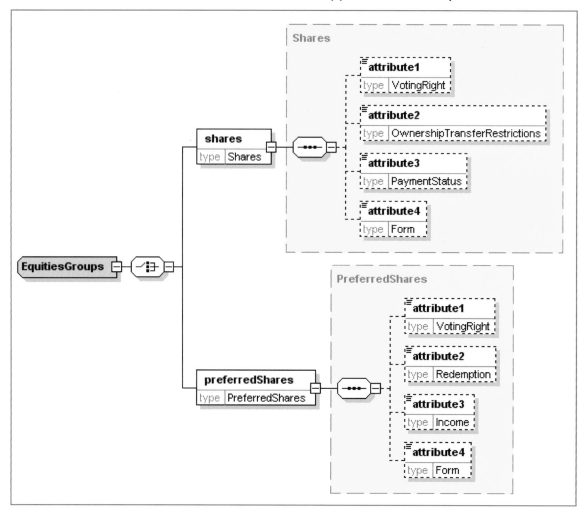

Figure 37. ISO 20022 XML generated from UML equivalent[15]

---

[15] Screenshot using the Altova® XMLSpy® XML editor

Semantic Metadata approach

The financial industry has been crying out for a standardised set of the building blocks, terms and definitions for master file and reference data for many years. Semantic modelling provides the ability to achieve this and the EDM Council has put substantial resources into developing a Semantic Repository and the Financial Industry Business Ontology (FIBO).

The first step in the development of the FIBO is the Wells Fargo's OTC Derivative products operational model Proof of Concept ("OTC PoC").This work has resulted in the creation of a number of ontologies including ones for representing OTC Interest Rate contracts, Legal Entity Identification and other common financial terms.

The tool used by for OTC PoC is Protégé, a free, open-source ontology editor.

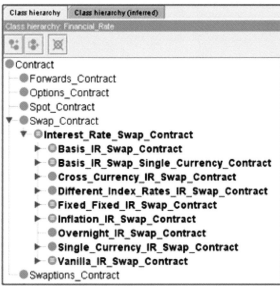

Figure 38. Product (contract) Hierarchy[16]

This semantic initiative has resulted in taxonomies able to identify specific end nodes, in Figure 33 specific product (or contract) types and Asset class in Figure 34 Asset classes.

Figure 39. Asset Class

When, however one is dealing with the multidimensional nature of financial products, one ends up with a cumbersome poly hierarchical model that comprises multiple ontology's that intersect at various points. This results in the same specific end node being assessable via multiple paths. This is difficult to implement into a production environment.

Digital Object Identifier and Classifications

The Digital Object Identifier (DOI®) was designed to support asset identification and has been included in this report, as it also enables definition of Metadata – an essential capability because an identifier is meaningless without its accompanying Metadata. Such information could include the Facets and Features inherent in a classification.

Vocabulary Mapping Framework

Given that there is a requirement to map between multiple classifications and identifiers, the Vocabulary Mapping Framework (VMF) extension of DOI® should be considered as it provides the ability to map and transform controlled vocabularies. VMF supports resource categories, versioning and party role concepts. In addition the facility to map to third party vocabularies is supplied. The VMF mapping tool is known as a VMF Matrix. As VMF is a vocabulary of SKOS, which in turn is a vocabulary of RDF, the reader needs to consider what the benefits the DOI/VMF framework offers.

---

[16] Screenshot using the Protégé ontology editor

Simple Knowledge Organization Systems (SKOS)

SKOS is a W3C recommendation and a vocabulary of RDF, designed for defining typologies, taxonomies, thesauri and classification schemes. It is a powerful framework that allows the user to define code lists, structured code lists and low level relationships at the Feature level as well as specific entries within a code lists. An ISO standard equivalent exists (ISO 25964), nonetheless is only supports a subset of the functionality that SKOS provides.

The example provided is a snippet or a scheme showing the representation of Sovereign debt and includes an Issuer type code list considered an important Facet in classifying securitized products. Please note that the ISITC and ISO CFI hierarchies have been concatenated into a single concept each to improve readability. The figure that follows is a graphical representation created using TopBraid Composer.

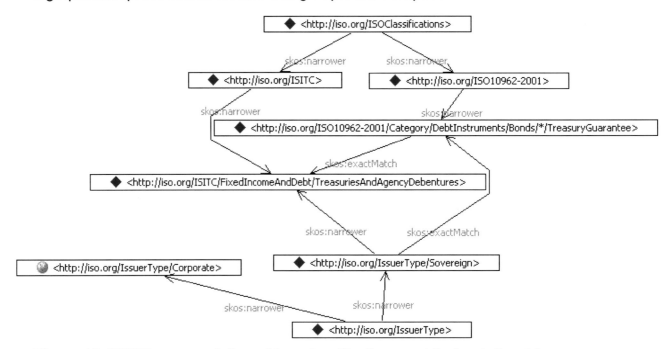

Figure 40. SKOS representation of two classifications and their relationships

Online references

ISO 20022 Repository & other material: www.iso20022.org/

Protégé ontology editor: protege.stanford.edu/

RDF Validator: http://www.w3.org/RDF/Validator/

SKOS: www.w3.org/2004/02/skos/

Sparx Systems Enterprise Architect: www.sparxsystems.com.au/

Topbraid Composer: www.topbraidcomposer.com/

Vocabulary Mapping Framework: www.doi.org/VMF/

94

Chapter 25

What is an appropriate scheme for financial products?

25. What is an appropriate scheme for financial products?

From the examination of the various industry classifications in this publication, it can be seen that there is a great deal of commonality in the approaches adopted by the industry. Asset class is normally at the top of any hierarchical tree. Another common facet used for grouping instruments is product type. Most applications use these two dimensions to identify the product groupings of interest, with a selection of further Features taken from an underlying pool, thus providing the capacity to identify specific product types.

Asset class and Base product Solution

The biggest advantage to this approach is that not only does it easily map to existing applications, it can also be easily integrated into an organization's existing trading data models.

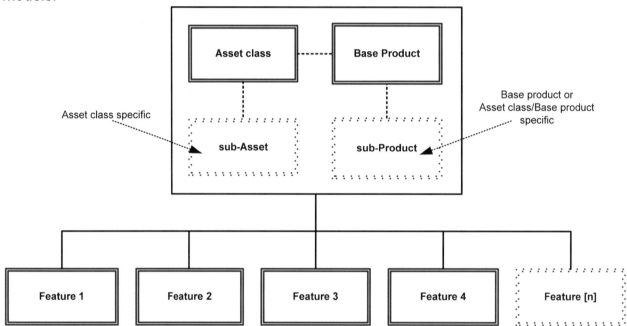

Figure 41. Asset class/Base product matrix classification scheme

These two dimensions result in the creation of a simple matrix, but to meet the requirements of the regulators and other enterprise-wide business processes, these primary facets sometimes need to be broken down to a second level of granularity.

Asset class / Base product

Asset class/Base product	Cap/Floor	Exotic	FRA	Forward	Future	Loan	Option	Security	Spot	Swap	Swaption	Warrant
Cash							X					
Credit				X[17]			X			X		
Commodity				X	X		X			X		
Equity		X		X	X	X	X	X		X		X
Foreign Exchange		X		X	X		X		X	X		X
Rate[18] (Interest, Inflation, …)	X	X	X	X	X	X	X	X		X	X	X
Hybrid (multiple Asset class)		X	X	X	X	X	X		X	X	X	X

It is worth highlighting that at present the ISDA proposal does not encompass Hybrid products, although it is understood that further work will be undertaken to expand the current asset class list to include them, but no timeline has been defined.

sub-Asset

The sub-Asset entries are Asset class specific and are principally based on the FpML Reporting Working Group proposal. This deviates from the ISDA proposal as the FpML focus is on classifying products, whilst the ISDA proposal aims to identify specific products. A classification approach based on the latter is less likely to be able to incorporate new financial products. A further drawback is that the ISDA proposal contains product features in its hierarchical structure.

Asset class	sub-Asset
Cash	Bullet Payment, Deposit , Lending, Repo, Reverse Repo, Security, …
Credit	Debt, Loan, Mortgage, Portfolio[19], Spread, …
Commodity	Agricultural, Economic, Energy, Environmental, Freight, Index, Industrial (e.g. Plastics), Insurance, Multi-Commodity Product, Precious Metals, Pulp & Paper, Real-estate, Weather
Equity	Mutual fund, Convertible bond, ..
ForeignExchange	Emerging Market Currencies, G10 Currencies , Non-deliverable Currencies
Rate (Single Currency)	Cross Currency, Debt, Inflation, Single Currency

sub-Product

sub-Product entries are Base product or Asset class/Base product specific and populated by selecting the appropriate information from the ISDA and FpML proposals.

Asset class/Base product	sub-Product
Credit/Swap	ABS, ABX, CDX, CDX Structured Tranche, Corporate, IOS, iTraxx, Loans, Sovereign, …
Equity/Swap	CFD, Correlation, Dividend, Portfolio[20], Price Return, Spreadbet, TRS, Variance, Volatility, …
Rate (Single Currency)/Swap	Fixed - Float, Fixed-Fixed, Basis, OIS, Variance
-/Option	Barrier, Binary/Digital[21], [Barrier & Binary/Digital]

---

[17] i.e. Credit Spread Forward, where the sub-Asset is set to Spread.
[18] ISDA proposes the use of "Interest Rate".
[19] Portfolio of single name credit default swaps.
[20] Return swap on a portfolio of CDS trades.
[21] ISDA proposal supports Barrier or Digital, not both.

Features

The use of Features has a dual purpose, firstly to identify specific product types and secondly to supply key information for an application to process a product appropriately.

An assessment of product features is required, with the aim of providing a firm semantic grounding to the classification. In particular, an evaluation of cash flows is recommended, for example the legs of swaps and swap style products. Please refer to the Equity derivative examples in Appendix C which include a high level assessment of the legs applicable to each product type.

Issuer Type

Given that the original aim of this publication was to focus on product typology, the scheme outlined in this section is appropriate to manage this goal, nonetheless it is appreciated that principally in the securitized world the type of Issuer/guarantor is also considered an important facet. This highlights the need to capture contractual differences dependent upon the type of issuer.

The possible entries for an Issuer type code list include:

- Charity,
- Corporate,
- Mutual,
- Partnership, and
- Sovereign.

Chapter 26

Recommendations and other considerations

26. Recommendations and other considerations

Having read this publication the reader will have obtained a better understanding of the financial product classifications landscape and the context within which each is used. They will also be able to appreciate how one can be constructed in a real business scenario and having examined various modelling methodologies will better understand which approach will best fit their own data architecture framework.

For a classification scheme to be of use to an organisation they need to be able to link it with a unique product identifier to multiple classifications. Will the ISIN and/or the ISDA UPI ever be able to fulfil this requirement? If not, would the next step be to extend the preferred classification such that with more Features it is able to develop a Symbology?"

ISO CFI Working Group

The ISO Working Group (TC68/SC4/WG6) is now in session and is keen to define a single classification to support the financial industry's current needs. It has been recognised that the current format and the ISO processes for maintenance and governance are not appropriate in the fast changing world of financial product development, especially given that the new regulatory frameworks are likely to spawn the creation of new products to comply with them. There is an opportunity for the ISO standard to become the über classification the world needs.

Regulatory impact considerations

The impact of regulations needs to be considered when constructing a classification. Not only is there likely to be a move away from Interest Rate Swaps and Swaptions, to hybrid products comprising both Futures and OTC components (i.e. Forward Interest Rate Swap Futures). The development of products to manage collateral is also expected. At the vanguard of the development of new standardised financial products is the Eris Exchange based in Chicago. For further information about this market, please visit: www.erisfutures.com

Recommendations

There are a number of observations that fall out of this analysis. These can be broken down under two subheadings, namely Scheme Design and Modelling Approach.

Scheme Design

Firstly, there are two key classification facets that occur regularly in most business applications. These two key dimensions are Asset class and Base product. It is also common for these facets to be broken down further into sub-Asset and sub-Product.

Secondly, the analysis also identified that the primary features important to systems relate to payout criteria and hence cash flows.

A third Facet may need to be considered for inclusion in a classification scheme principally when dealing with securitized instruments. This relates to the need to identify the type of Issuer (Sovereign, Corporate, etc...) and hence to capture contractual differences dependent upon them.

Modelling Approach

Keep it simple should always be the philosophy. The key requirements for any classification framework or metadata model should include the capabilities to support:

- code lists

- hierarchical dependencies or structured code lists

- poly hierarchies

- low level relationships, this should include the ability to link specific entries within code lists.

- versioning and change control

Of all the frameworks examined in this publication only SKOS seems to meet all the requirements and is specifically designed for representing thesauri, typologies, taxonomies and classifications. In addition, it can be mapped onto the ISO standard equivalent, though the ISO standard, 25964 only supports a subset of the SKOS functions.

Contact the Author

If you have any queries or wish to discuss this subject, feel free to drop a line to the author at:

msexton@londonmarketsystems.com

This page has been intentionally left blank.

Appendices

Appendix A - Consultation submissions to the regulators

A1 Consultation on the Regulation on OTC Derivatives, CCPs & SDRs

www.esma.europa.eu/content/London-Market-Systems-1

A2 The Quest to classify OTC Derivative Instruments – Feb-09

www.esma.europa.eu/system/files/LMS_OTC_Classifcationv1_3.pdf

Appendix B - Glossary

Asset class	A group of financial products that exhibit similar characteristics and behaviour in the marketplace as well as being subject to the same laws and regulations. From an ISDA perspective the Asset classes are identified as: - Credit - Equity - Interest Rate - FX - Energy, Commodities, Developing Products - Structured Products and other products
Attribute	A specific definition or value, possibly a contractual definition, such as a strike price or the currency associated with a cash flow/leg.
Base product	A financial product or contract type grouping. (i.e. Futures, Options, Forwards, Swaptions, etc...)
Characteristic	Can be either a Facet or a Feature.
Classification	See Product classification.
Code list	An approved list of options for a specific Characteristic (sometimes referred to controlled vocabulary). A Code list might be human readable, in abbreviated form or enumerated codes.
Facet	"A clearly defined, mutually exclusive, and collectively exhaustive aspects, properties or characteristics of a class or specific subject"[22] An example of this could be categorising by Asset class.
Feature	A characteristic of a financial product or an external facet that is used to categorise a financial product. It may be derived from multiple attributes of a financial product.
Financial product/ instrument	This encompasses securities, derivative instruments and other products (i.e. loans) associated with the trading activities of an organisation.
Product classification	An analysis of products which may include product specific Features and external influences, such as Business context. An example of an external influence could be how the instrument is traded; a convertible bond for example is traded as an equity. However, at times of default, holders would probably wish to categorize such products as a debt instrument, since they would become creditors.
Product Typology	The classification of financial products according to structural features.
RDF	Standing for Resource Description Framework, it is the standard for encoding metadata and other semantic understanding.
Security	A standardised financial product, such as sovereign debt, exchange traded equities or derivatives.
SKOS	Or Simple Knowledge Organization Systems (KOS) it is a vocabulary of RDF specifically designed to represent typologies, taxonomies, thesauri and classification schemes.
UPI	Unique Product Identifier, such as the ISDA UPI proposal that comprises of a product identifier and an accompanying classification scheme.

---

[22] Taylor, A. G. (1992). Introduction to Cataloging and Classification. 8th edition Englewood, Colorado: Libraries Unlimited.

Appendix C – Asset class and Base product examples

In addition to the two dimensional approach (Asset class and Product) the key Features can be used to drill down into specific product types; these are examined in the following examples.

Equity Derivative examples

Key Features

Product Type	Asset	Base product	sub-Product		Underlyer	Delivery	Payoff Frequency	Payoff Currency Type	Legs
Contract for Difference	Equity	Swap	CFD		Index	Cash	Periodically	Domestic	Margin on underlyer appreciation & tax vs. Interest & margin on underlyer deprecation.
Spreadbet	Equity	Swap	Spreadbet		Single Name	Cash	On Expiry	Domestic	Margin on underlyer appreciation vs. Margin on underlyer deprecation.
TRS	Equity	Swap	TRS		Index	Cash	Periodically	Domestic	Underlyer appreciation & dividends vs. Interest & Underlyer deprecation
Price Return Swap	Equity	Swap	Price Return		Single Name	Cash	Periodically	Domestic	Underlyer appreciation vs. Interest & Underlyer deprecation
Variance	Equity[23]	Swap	Variance		Single Name	Cash	On Expiry	Domestic	Strike price vs. Variance from strike price

---

[23] Variance Swaps are not always Equity based.

Appendix D - Further Reading and References

1. Aaron J. Loehrlein 'Hierarchical Organization Structures' (January 2012)

2. Bank of International Settlements - Guide to the international financial statistics (2009)

3. Commodity Futures Trading Commission - 17 CFR Part 43 Real-Time Public Reporting of Swap Transaction Data (Jan 2012)

4. ESB Statistical Classification of Financial Markets Instruments (2005)

5. EUSIPA DERIVATIVE MAP (2009)

6. ISDA Implementation Plan for Unique Product Identifiers (June 2011)

7. ISDA OTC Taxonomies Rules of Operations (December 2011)

8. ISITC Classification Code List (2011)

9. ISO 10962 - Securities and related financial instruments — Classification of Financial Instruments (CFI code) (2001)

10. ISO/TS 20022-3:2004 UNIversal Financial Industry message scheme -- Part 3: ISO 20022 modelling guidelines

11. ISO/TS 20022-4:2004 UNIversal Financial Industry message scheme -- Part 4: ISO 20022 XML design rules

12. London Market Systems Limited, MiFID Alternative Instrument Identifier (2007)

13. Martin C. Sexton – ISITC Europe Quarterly Meeting Presentation, "Can an industry-wide instrument classification ever hit the spot?" (July 2010)

14. Nassim Talib (1997) 'Dynamic Hedging, Managing vanilla and exotic Options' - Wiley Finance

15. SDMX Standards: Section 1 - Framework for SDMX Technical Standards - Version 2.1 (2011)

16. Taylor, A. G. (1992) 'Introduction to Cataloging and Classification' - Englewood, Colorado: Libraries Unlimited.

Online References

Given the risk of online references becoming obsolete, it is recommended that the reader goes to the following web page to obtain up-to-date links and other material of interest:

www.londonmarketsystems.com/classifications

This page has been intentionally left blank.

Index

Index

ISITC, 21, 40, 41, 107
ISO 10962, 6, 8, 12, 18, 19, 21, 36, 86, 88, 107
ISO 200022, 40
ISO 20022 methodology, 91
ISO 6166, 12, 18
ISO CFI, 6, 9, 18, 21, 24, 27, 30, 36, 40, 88, 91, 100
ISO Working Group (TC68/SC4/WG6), 19, 100
iTraxx, 97

L

Legs, 106
Loans, 36, 46, 66, 97
London Market Systems, 24, 107

M

Milieu Layer, 3
Mortgage, 8, 36, 97
Mutual funds, 46

N

NYSE.Liffe exchange, 8

O

OASIS Genericode, 86
ontologies, 93
Option type, 8
Order of Option, 90

P

Path Dependent, 90
Payoff Currency Type, 106
Payoff Frequency, 106
poly hierarchical, 7, 93
poly-hierarchical, 7, 68
Price Return Swap, 106

R

Regulation 144A, 8

Regulation S, 8
Regulatory impact, 100
Repo, 37, 66, 97
RIXML, 16, 66

S

SDMX, 87, 107
Semantic Repository, 68, 93
settlement and reconciliation, 40, 41
Spreadbet, 62, 97, 106
Statistical Data and Metadata Exchange, 87
strict hierarchical, 7, 86
Strict Hierarchy, 7
structured products, 44, 57, 105
sub-Asset, 52, 57, 58, 97, 100
sub-Product, 10, 60, 68, 97, 100, 106
Swaps Data (trade) Repositories ("SDR"s), 52
Swaptions, 32, 97
SWIFT messages, 41
symbology, 3, 12, 100

T

Taxonomies, 2, 3, 60, 87, 107
Time Homogenous, 89
TRS, 62, 97, 106
Typology, 2, 3, 105

U

UML, 86, 88, 89, 91, 92
Unique Product Identifier (UPI), 12, 56, 60

V

Variance, 28, 58, 97, 106
Vocabulary Mapping Framework (VMF), 93

X

xor constraint, 88

CPSIA information can be obtained at www.ICGtesting.com
Printed in the USA
LVIW01n2342280817
546689LV00003B/27